Windows® 8 Kickstart

About the Author

James Russell has built, and repaired PCs and installed, configured, and debugged most versions of Windows from Windows 95 to Windows 8. A long-time editor and writer of technical books for various publishers, he is currently integrating social media strategy into a career focus, and was recently named by Mashable.com as one of 101 social media experts to follow on Google+. James currently writes and edits technical articles for Web sites such as AZCentral and eHow Tech as part of his duties for Demand Media Studios, where he focuses on technical topics including Windows, Office, and Android devices. He has significant experience with the Mozilla open-source project since Mozilla's M4 milestone in 1999 (having been responsible for Mozilla .6's / Netscape 6's View > Themes menu) and has also rewritten the Linux, Windows, and Mac release notes as well as the README files for Mozilla's .6 and 1.0 versions.

About the Technical Editor

Seth Rosenblatt is a Senior Editor at CNET and wrote CNET's official review of Windows 8. He also covers browsers, security, and privacy, the intersection of tech and pop culture, and creates tech-flavored galleries from his photos. After traveling the world, he currently lives in San Francisco with two dogs, five roommates, and a motorcycle.

Windows® 8 Kickstart

James Howard Russell

New York   Chicago   San Francisco
Lisbon   London   Madrid   Mexico City
Milan   New Delhi   San Juan
Seoul   Singapore   Sydney   Toronto

Cataloging-in-Publication Data is on file with the Library of Congress

McGraw-Hill books are available at special quantity discounts to use as premiums and sales promotions, or for use in corporate training programs. To contact a representative, please e-mail us at bulksales@mcgraw-hill.com.

Windows® 8 Kickstart

1 2 3 4 5 6 7 8 9 0   DOC/DOC   1 0 9 8 7 6 5 4 3 2

ISBN   978-0-07-180582-7
MHID   0-07-180582-6

SPONSORING EDITOR	**TECHNICAL EDITOR**	**PRODUCTION SUPERVISOR**
Megg Morin	Seth Rosenblatt	Jean Bodeaux
EDITORIAL SUPERVISOR	**COPY EDITOR**	**COMPOSITION**
Jody McKenzie	Mike McGee	Cenveo Publisher Services
PROJECT MANAGER	**PROOFREADERS**	**ILLUSTRATION**
Vasundhara Sawhney, Cenveo Publisher Services	Claire Splan and Joshua Chase	Cenveo Publisher Services
ACQUISITIONS COORDINATOR	**INDEXER**	**ART DIRECTOR, COVER**
Stephanie Evans	Karin Arrigoni	Jeff Weeks

*To my mother Jacquelyn Arlene Cordoza
and my father John Howard Russell*

Love always

CONTENTS AT A GLANCE

CONTENTS

heck Out Receipt

ewmarket Public Library
05--953-5110
ww.newmarketpl.ca

riday, Jul 4 2014 4:04PM
2343
ASIVARNAM, VEERABADRAN

tem: 35923003551829
itle: Word 2013 for dummies
all no.: 005.52 Micro-G COPY 1
aterial: Book
ue: 25/07/2014

tem: 35923003402171
itle: Window 8 kickstart
all no.: 005.446 Rus c.1
aterial: Book
ue: 25/07/2014

otal items: 2

ACKNOWLEDGMENTS

I have many people to thank in regards to this book, including most notably the single-greatest tech book agent in the business, Carole Jelen at Waterside Productions, who got me the project, and Megg Morin, the sponsoring editor who trusted me to write my own Windows 8 book as part of a brand new series and midwifed the chapters and table of contents in collaboration with myself and technical editor Seth "my dog huffs glue" Rosenblatt of CNET. Thanks also to the book's acquisitions coordinator, Stephanie Evans, the project manager at Cenveo, Vasundhara Sawhney, and the copy editor, Mike McGee.

I also want to thank Microsoft—and in particular John Yarborough of Microsoft's PR team—for helping me figure out a new lexicon for Windows to use in the book and for sending me the final version of Windows on a USB stick so I could finish the book in time for the release of Windows.

Thanks also to Justin Wood and other Mozilla folks who helped me figure out I wasn't going to be able to cover the Windows Store versions of Firefox (or Chrome) because they wouldn't be ready in time for the book's early release. And a special thanks to Jesse Stay—after editing his *Google+ For Dummies, Portable Edition* and *Google+ Marketing For Dummies*, I will attribute any recognition this book receives on social networks to knowledge I've gotten from Jesse.

There are also some folks who didn't help in the direct creation of the book but who significantly aided me in my ability to finish it: John Molina and his mother Nancy Ciarrocchi, Garrett Mallory, Suzan Barroso and her son A. J. Barroso, my sister Julie Mae Donovan, my uncle David W. Russell, my stepfather Paul Richard Grenek, my godmother Deana Burnam McKettrick, Jolynn Shaffer, Shane Hutton, and Josh "Joshie" Chase.

Thanks also to Aaron Michael Bordner, his parents John and Cindy Mosqueda, Jennifer "Boriss" Morrow, Majken "Lucy" Connor, and David Youhanna.

Thanks also to Leah Michael, Kathryn Bourgouine, Kyle Looper, Jodi Jensen, and Jade Leah Williams for helping me grow as an editor and a writer over the years.

INTRODUCTION

Windows 8 is the biggest design overhaul to the Windows interface in recent memory, and with this major change in technology comes a major need for information about it. If you're reading this book, you have in your hands the know-how to make your transition to Microsoft's new operating system smooth and enjoyable. I'll show you what's the same as in Windows 7, what has moved and where it went to, and offer tips and tricks that will get you up and running with Windows 8 in no time. If you're like me, you'll love the new operating system so much that going back to a Windows 7 machine will actually disappoint you.

In this introduction, I'll get you up to speed on the specifics of this book, what's in it, and how to navigate it with ease.

My Assumptions About You

To avoid writing an encyclopedia on the subject and help me focus the content of this book, I have made a few assumptions about you, the reader. I have assumed, firstly, that you have at least used Windows or a Mac in the past and that you most likely have surfed the Web, used productivity software of some sort—be it e-mail, Microsoft Office apps, or printing. Finally, I have assumed that you probably haven't used Windows 8 before—or anything like it—since this book is coming out at the same time as Windows 8 itself.

Note that one thing I did not assume, like most previous books on Windows, is that you're using a keyboard and a mouse. For the first time ever, you can use Windows on a touchscreen tablet—such as the Microsoft Surface—with ease, and I have worked with Microsoft to draft and create the lexicon for this book so I can cover both keyboard and mouse operations in addition to touchscreen functions.

How to Navigate this Book

Aside from the Contents at a Glance page, the table of contents, and the index, this book is organized into three parts to help you get the information you need the fastest:

- **Part I**   In this part, I show you the very basics of using Windows, from navigating the new Start screen and desktop to showing you how to configure Windows, work with your files, and keep Windows not only secure from malware but up to date as well.

- **Part II**   This section showcases information on where to find Windows Store apps—the brightly colored tiles on the Start screen—from managing and downloading apps to using those same apps to view, manage, and watch movies; listen to music; view photos; communicate with others via instant messaging or various social networks; and download, install, and use other Windows Store apps such as games.

- **Part III**   Office productivity is part of the Windows legacy, and this section of the book covers using your Windows 8 device with other devices—such as printers—and helps get you set up with Office 2013, which has been re-created with Windows 8 in mind and integrates into the Windows 8 experience beautifully.

Where to Go from Here

This book is bigger than just the pages between these covers. I have created both a Google+ page and a Facebook page for the book so I can keep updating you after the book is published and as more software comes out—thus giving you access to extra information as it becomes available.

You can access the book's Facebook page by going to www.facebook .com/Windows8Kickstart or entering "Windows 8 Kickstart" (without quotes) in the Search field at the top of the Facebook page. The book's Google+ page can be found at https://plus.google.com/u/0/s/Windows%20 8%20Kickstart or by entering "+Windows 8 Kickstart" (without quotes) in the Google Plus search box. I'll include similar, but not always identical, information on both pages. If you have questions about the book or (egad!) notice something wrong, e-mail me at jhrussell@outlook.com.

Conventions Used in this Book

Now You Know   The Now You Know sidebars provide deeper detail on a topic or specifics for accomplishing a task.

 Tip   Tips help you make the most of Windows 8 by offering shortcuts or ways to streamline and super-charge your Windows 8 experience.

 Note   Notes aim to draw your attention to supplemental information, background steps, or additional hardware or software requirements.

 Caution   Keep a sharp eye out for the Caution icon to help you steer clear of potential pitfalls or problems that may lie ahead.

Part I

Orient Yourself to Windows 8

1

Start Up Windows 8

Welcome, friend, to Windows 8! For the first time since Windows 95, Microsoft has redefined the Windows interface in dramatic fashion to make the operating system more user friendly and to incorporate navigational tools that are appropriate for touchscreen interfaces such as tablets. The new interface takes a little getting used to, but after you're up and running you'll most likely start to really enjoy and appreciate the new interface and features.

When you first start Windows 8, the operating system prompts you for information to allow you to configure it and make it your own. Luckily, the process is pretty painless, and in just a few minutes you'll be ready to go with your new system. In this chapter, you'll learn everything you need to know to start using Windows 8 and its new, overhauled interface. You'll need to create an account, configure how you want Windows to work, and then sign in to your account to start using Windows. Later chapters in Part I will cover additional information about fine-tuning your Windows 8 configuration, getting your computer customized, and setting up devices.

Configure Windows 8 So You Can Use It

When you first start your Windows 8 system, you'll have to choose a name for your computer, create an account name and password, and choose either to use the default Microsoft settings or custom settings to configure how you want Windows 8 to run, among other things.

Following are a few things to keep in mind as you configure Windows 8 before first use:

- The choices in Custom Settings are pretty benign, but privacy hounds may want to disable them.

- If you use an @outlook.com, @msn.com, @live.com, or @hotmail .com address, Microsoft will even be able to sync and back up your settings, including:

  - Browsing history

  - Bookmarks

  - Settings in Internet Explorer 10

  - Some application settings

  - Office 2013 settings

  - Desktop color and theme

  - Login options

 Outlook.com accounts are by far the best option for a Microsoft account, with a sleek, clean interface, 7 gigabytes of SkyDrive space, and Web versions of Word, Excel, and PowerPoint built in. See Chapter 14 for help getting or transferring your existing Microsoft account to an @outlook.com account.

- Passwords are becoming passé compared to passphrases: stringing four random words together in a phrase with correct grammar is actually far more difficult for a computer to guess than a cryptic single pass "word" is. For example, "bottle shirt smoke cat."

- Your computer's name cannot include certain characters or spaces. If you type in an illegal character, Windows will alert you and list all of the forbidden characters (see Table 1-1).

{	|	}	~	[	\
]	^	'	:	;	<
=	>	?	@	!	"
#	$	%	`	(	)
+	/	.	,	*	&

Table 1-1 *Forbidden characters for a PC name*

- Using Express Settings is certainly shorter than setting up and using a Microsoft account, but if you want access to some of the really cool features in Windows 8, such as Sync, use a Microsoft account.

- Enabling Windows Update is a good idea. The service has improved dramatically in recent versions of Windows and when enabled it can significantly improve the security of your computer and help ensure you access the new Windows 8 features sooner rather than later.

- Setting parental controls is a different process than setting content filters. Microsoft has included reasonably robust parental controls in Windows 8. See Chapter 5 for more information.

Sign In to Windows 8

After configuring Windows, Windows 8 creates your account and lets you sign in to your new account. The process of signing in to Windows 8 can be customized more than ever before.

 Besides using a Microsoft account like an @outlook.com, @hotmail.com, @msn.com, or @live.com e-mail account, you can also set up a four-digit PIN number or log in by drawing on a photo of your choice (see Chapter 2).

The first thing you'll see prior to inputting your account e-mail and password is a full-screen photograph, as shown in Figure 1-1. By default, the photo is overlaid with the time, date, power level, and an icon showing your network status. Here's how to sign in to Windows 8 for the first time.

1. Press the SPACEBAR to dismiss the full-screen photo if using a keyboard, or swipe your finger up from the bottom of the screen if you're using a tablet.

2. Type your password into the text field (your e-mail is already listed in the upper text box).

3. Press ENTER.

Figure 1-1 *Your sign-in screen is behind a full-screen photograph.*

 You'll be able to change the image in your settings later (see Chapter 2).

The Brand New Start Screen

After signing in to your account for the first time, Windows configures your account settings and summons the new Start screen. The color of this screen depends on the color you chose when configuring your computer; the default color is blue. Against this colored background, you see a bunch of colored boxes that Microsoft calls *tiles* staring back at you. Like apps, each tile is an icon that you can click or tap to run the program.

To kickstart your Windows 8 installation, you need to understand the key differences between the Windows 8–style user interface and the desktop interface, with which you're already familiar if you've used previous versions of Windows. Key features new to Windows 8 include:

- The Start screen
- Tiles
- Charms
- The modified desktop
- Tablet navigation

The following sections give you information on the differences between the Windows 8–style user interface and the desktop interface so you can get up and running with Windows 8 fast.

The Windows 8–Style Interface

With Windows 8, Microsoft has created a new user interface that started on Windows Phone 7.5 (Microsoft has said the next Xbox will have a similar tiled interface). Think of the Start screen as a full-screen version of the classic Windows Start menu—all of the same features are available, they're just in different locations on the interface.

 You can summon the Start screen from anywhere by pressing the WINDOWS key.

As you can see in Figure 1-2, Microsoft has highlighted some features of the Start screen by displaying them on brightly colored tiles. These brighter tiles indicate Windows 8–style apps that are new to Windows 8 and are significantly different than classic Windows applications. Tiles with a dark blue background (none of which are present in Figure 1-2—you have to scroll to the right to see them) represent familiar desktop applications that work on the Windows 8 desktop. You will also see a tile for the desktop in the lower left corner

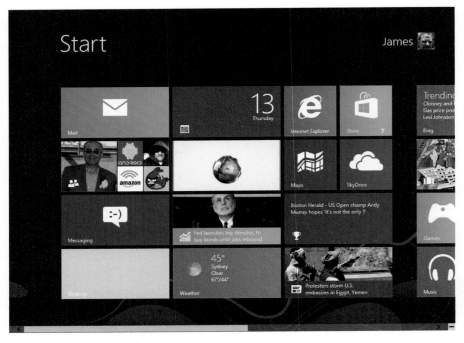

Figure 1-2   *The Windows 8 Start screen*

of the Start screen. Some of the larger tiles are visually active and display up-to-date information. For example, the Weather app shows the latest weather, while the Messaging app shows your latest instant messages. Simply click or tap on a tile to access the app.

 The ENTER key is tied to the top-left tile on the Start screen, so if you put the Desktop tile in the upper left you can toggle between the Start screen and desktop by pressing the WINDOWS key and ENTER key, respectively.

Default Tiles Highlight Microsoft Services

Microsoft has a history of bundling features in newer versions of Windows that used to be part of separate applications. Internet Explorer was the first such bundled application in Windows 98 and Windows Media Player soon followed in Windows 98 SE. With Windows 8, Microsoft is taking bundling to a whole new level. Windows 8 bundles the following:

- Facebook, Twitter, LinkedIn, Flickr, and Skype
- The Bing search engine
- Bing Maps
- Bing Weather
- Xbox Games
- SkyDrive cloud storage
- Windows Store
- The Music app
- The Video app

Together, the last three bullets listed here represent the components of Microsoft's answer to Apple's iTunes and the Google Play Store. The company also requires you to use a Microsoft account, much as Google makes you use a Google account for Android devices. The account can't be just any Windows Live account but must be one that specifically uses an @outlook.com, @msn.com, @hotmail.com, or @live.com e-mail address, thus letting you access some of the new features in Windows 8, such as Sync.

Navigate the Windows 8 Desktop

On the Start screen, you will see a large tile for your desktop in the lower left. Click or tap it to summon the desktop. The familiar Windows interface and taskbar appear, as shown in Figure 1-3, but don't be deceived. There's a lot that's new in this revamped Windows desktop.

Recycle Bin

Desktop

Quick Launch Bar   Taskbar   System Tray

Figure 1-3 *The desktop looks familiar—but there's a lot that's new about it.*

The various parts of the desktop are as follows:

- **Desktop**   All of your windows will appear here.
- **Recycle Bin**   Drop something in here to delete it. Right-click it and choose Empty Recycle Bin to permanently delete all items in it.
- **Taskbar**   Shows all open windows.
- **System Tray**   Shows the clock, time, and tiny icons notifying you of what's running in the background on your system.
- **Quick Launch Bar**   The left side of the taskbar has icons that give you easy access to programs you use a lot.

 By default, Internet Explorer and File Explorer are the only icons shown here, but you can right-click any desktop app icon and choose Pin to Taskbar to add it as well.

The Start Menu Is Now the Start Screen

The first thing you're likely to notice on the new desktop is that the Start button is not on the left corner of the taskbar. If you hover your mouse in the lower left corner of the screen, you will see a Start button that you can click to summon the Start screen. As mentioned earlier, the Start screen is new in Windows 8 and encompasses most of the features that were formerly on the Start menu. On a tablet, you swipe in from the left edge an inch or so and then swipe your finger back to the left edge—essentially doing a U-turn with your finger. This summons the Start button, as shown in Figure 1-4, as well as a list of any open applications. Tap the Start button to access the Start screen.

Use Edges or Corners to Access Features

The Windows 8 screen includes four interactive screen edges. On a non-touchscreen PC, these "edges" are actually hot spots in the four corners of the screen that you hover your mouse over to access.

Figure 1-4   *The Start button*

Hot spots summon key features of the Windows 8 user interface. You activate them by hovering your mouse cursor over the appropriate corner of the screen or by swiping in from the correct direction on a tablet.

The hot spots on the Windows 8 interface are accessible regardless of which app you're using or whether you're in the desktop or Start screen. The following sections delve deeper into the Windows 8 hot spots and charms.

The Charms

Move your mouse into the extreme upper right or lower right corner of the screen to summon a bar that has five icons on it that Microsoft calls *charms*, as shown in Figure 1-5. When you hover your mouse over these icons, the bar's background turns black and you can also see the time and date on the left side of the screen. If you're using a Windows 8 tablet, simply swipe in from the right side of the screen with your finger to access the charms.

 Summon the charms by pressing and holding down the WINDOWS key and pressing the c key.

In order from top to bottom, the five charm icons are as follows:

- **Search** Summons the Search sidebar on the Start screen. From here you can search apps, files, and settings by clicking the appropriate item below the search box. Below those choices you can click to search more specific types of files or even the Internet by clicking Video to search videos, Photos to search photos, Internet Explorer to search the Internet, and so on.

- **Share** View any share options for the currently running app.

Figure 1-5   *The Windows 8 charms*

- **Start**   Takes you to the Start screen.

- **Devices**   Brings up a list of your devices; click a device to view options for it. This is how you print in Windows 8–style apps. See Chapter 13 for more information about setting up and working with your printers and devices.

- **Settings**   Brings up a sidebar on the right side of your screen that includes links at the top for the Control Panel, Personalization, PC Info, and Help. At the bottom of the sidebar you'll see icons for your network, volume, brightness, notifications, power, and keyboard. Below that is a Change PC Settings link that you can click to bring up the Settings app, which includes many more settings you can choose from. See Chapter 2 for more information about configuring your settings.

The Task Switcher

The second of the three Windows 8 hot spots is the task switcher, which gives you easy access to your most recently used Windows 8–style programs. You can think of the task switcher as sort of a taskbar, for Windows 8–style apps. Move your mouse into the extreme upper left corner of the screen to access a black box area that shows your last-used application as shown in Figure 1-6. Move down from there to view more previously used applications. If you're using a Windows 8 tablet, simply swipe in from the left edge of the screen to see your recent applications or swipe in from the left edge an inch or so and then swipe your finger back to the left edge to summon the task switcher with the Start button at the bottom.

You can click or tap an application or drag it to the middle of the screen to switch to it. You can also drag and drop it—Microsoft calls this *snapping* an app—to the left or right of the screen so you can view

Figure 1-6   *The task switcher*

both applications alongside one another. If you do so, a vertical bar with dots in the middle of it will appear between apps, allowing you to grab it and drag it to make either application take up most of the screen, while the other takes up just a small portion of it. You can also hover at the upper edge of the screen when in a Windows 8–style app; a hand will appear indicating that you can click and drag the app to snap it left or right or drag the app to the bottom of the screen to close it.

 You can only snap apps if your resolution is at least 1366 × 768.

The New Start Button

The Start button is a tile-like thumbnail of the Start screen. Clicking or tapping it brings up the Start screen while on the desktop or within a Windows 8–style application. If you access the button while on the Start screen, a thumbnail of your desktop will appear instead. Move your mouse into the lower left corner of your screen to access the button or swipe in from the left an inch or so and then swipe back to the left edge. Click or tap the button to switch to the Start screen from the desktop or a Windows 8–style application.

Your Applications Are All Here

To find all of your apps, summon the Start screen by pressing the WINDOWS key or by moving your mouse into the lower left corner of the desktop and clicking the Start button. Then, right-click an empty spot on the Start screen and click the All Apps icon that appears in a bar along the bottom of the screen, or, if using a tablet, swipe up from the bottom of the Start screen and tap the All Apps icon. Figure 1-7 shows the default apps screen.

Figure 1-7 *All of your applications on one screen*

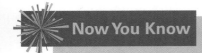 **Place Apps on the Start Screen or Desktop Taskbar**

Navigating to the All Apps screen is not the easiest way to access an application that you use regularly. Any app listed on the All Apps screen can be added to the Start screen, but only desktop apps can be added to the desktop's taskbar. Here's how to add an app to either: From the Start screen, right-click your mouse on an empty spot of the screen or swipe up from the bottom edge on a tablet and then choose All Apps from the bar that appears on the bottom. Then, simply find and right-click, or press and hold, the tile for the app or feature you want easier access to and choose Pin to Start or Pin to Taskbar. From the desktop, right-click any icon and choose Pin to Start or Pin to Taskbar from the context menu.

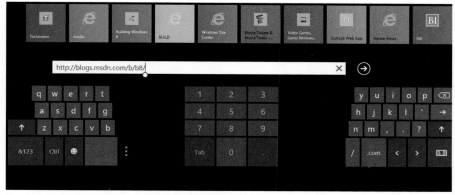

Used with permission from Microsoft Corporation.

Figure 1-8   *The Windows 8 tablet onscreen keyboard*

Use the Onscreen Keyboard

Microsoft has included an onscreen keyboard for Windows 8 tablets. You have two keyboards and a stylus option you can switch between using the button that has a keyboard on it in the lower right. One keyboard overlays the whole screen; the second, shown in Figure 1-8, is split, with half of the letters in the lower left corner, the number pad in the center, and the other half of the letters in the lower right so you can use your thumbs to type while you hold the tablet. To summon the keyboard, simply tap into a text field.

Navigate Your Files with File Explorer

File Explorer is such a key part of working with files and folders in Windows that I've given it its own chapter (see Chapter 4).

Use the Control Panel to Configure Your Computer

No matter what app you're in or whether you're on the desktop or the Start screen, you can access the venerable Control Panel, shown in Figure 1-9, in several ways.

Figure 1-9 *Control all aspects of your computer with the Control Panel.*

Microsoft has a history of allowing multiple ways to perform various tasks in their software depending on user preference. Which methods are "best" depends on the user and even the context of where the user is in the interface. If you're on the desktop, the first method is probably easiest, but if you're on the Start screen, it's faster to use search.

The following sections show you the various ways you can access the Control Panel.

Summon the Control Panel from the Old Start Menu

The Start menu is sort of still there, and this is one of the fastest ways to access the Control Panel. Here's how to bring up the Control Panel from the old Start menu:

1. To access the Start button, hover your mouse cursor in the lower left corner of the screen or swipe in from the left an inch and swipe back to the edge.

2. Right-click the Start button or press down on it for a few seconds if you're using a tablet.

3. Choose Control Panel from the menu that appears.

Summon the Control Panel from the All Apps Screen

Here's how to bring up the Control Panel from the All Apps screen:

1. Hover your mouse cursor in the lower left corner of the screen and click the Start button to access the Start screen. On a tablet, swipe in from the left edge an inch or so and then swipe back to the left edge and tap the Start button.

2. Right-click and choose All Apps from the bar that appears on the bottom. If you're using a tablet, swipe up from the bottom of the screen to access the bar.

3. Find and click or tap the Control Panel tile.

Summon the Control Panel from Search

The Windows Control Panel can be easily accessed by searching for it; Windows 8 has the same powerful search capabilities that Windows 7 and Windows Vista had on the Start menu—and more. To access the Control Panel from search, follow these steps:

1. Hover your mouse cursor in the extreme upper right or lower right corners of the screen or swipe in from the right edge and click or tap the Search charm.

2. Type "Control Panel" into the search bar.

3. Click the Control Panel tile that appears on the left.

Sign Out of Windows 8

When you're finished using your computer, you'll need to sign out of your account so others can use it or before you shut it down. To sign out of Windows 8, from the Start screen click your username and choose Sign Out from the drop-down menu.

Shut Off, Restart, or Put Your Computer to Sleep

Periodically, you'll have to restart your computer to complete application or Windows update installations. You also may want to put your computer to sleep or simply shut it down when you're not going to be using it. You have two options when you want to shut off, restart, or put your computer to sleep—these pertain to when you're still signed in and after you're signed out.

 Before shutting off, restarting, or putting your computer to sleep whether you're signed in or not, it's best to shut down open applications and save your work to avoid data loss.

Shut Off, Restart, or Put Your Computer to Sleep While Signed In

Here's how to sign out of Windows while signed in:

1. Hover your mouse cursor in the extreme upper right or lower right corners of the screen and access the Settings charm.
2. Click or tap the Power button.
3. Choose Restart, Shut Down, or Sleep.

Shut Off, Restart, or Put Your Computer to Sleep When Signed Out

Here's how to shut off, restart, or put your PC to sleep after signing out of Windows:

1. Press the SPACEBAR or swipe up from the bottom of the screen.
2. Click or tap the Power button in the lower right corner of the screen.
3. Choose Restart, Shut Down, or Sleep.

2

Configure Your Start Screen and Customize Your Settings

Possibly the most obvious of the new features in Windows 8 is the new Start screen, which displays the Windows 8–style tile setup. If you have a Windows Phone 7.5 or later, you will be familiar with this interface; otherwise, the interface will look different than anything you've ever seen for a Windows operating system interface.

The Windows 8 Start screen replaces the Windows desktop and its old Start menu as the jumping off place for everything Windows—now, all of your apps are accessible from it. I introduced you to navigating the Start screen and what tiles are in Chapter 1. In this chapter, I'll go more in depth and show you how to make the Start screen yours by manipulating your tiles and customizing the display settings for the Start screen itself. After that, I'll shift gears slightly and show you how to adjust Windows' settings in general.

Manipulate Tiles on the Start Screen

If the default tiles don't reflect your preferences 100 percent, that's okay. Windows 8 allows you to add, remove, and move tiles, navigate the Start screen, and change your settings. The following sections show you how.

Add Tiles

You can easily add tiles to programs and features that you want quick access to. To add a tile for a program, follow these steps:

1. Right-click or press and hold on an empty portion of the Start screen.

2. Select All Apps, which appears on a bar in the lower portion of the screen.

3. Right-click or press and hold on the app you want to add a tile for and choose Pin to Start.

 If you are using a mouse that has a scroll wheel and there are too many apps for you to see them all on one screen, scroll down on your wheel to move the screen to the right. Similarly, scroll the wheel up to move back to the left. On a touchscreen device, just swipe your finger right or left instead. This works in tile applications as well, such as when in the Video, Music, Weather, or Games apps.

Delete Tiles

To delete a tile you don't want taking up space on your Start screen, simply right-click or press and hold the tile and choose Unpin from Start to get rid of it.

Move Tiles

Moving tiles is as simple as dragging and dropping them on the Start screen to where you want them. Other tiles will automatically rearrange themselves to accommodate the dropped one. Continue dragging and dropping tiles as you desire—for example, if you install a new app and have added it as a tile to your Start screen, it adds itself to the right side of the screen. You can drag it and drop it in the upper left for easier access if you choose to.

The next section shows you how to customize the settings for the Start screen itself, not just the tiles on it.

Customize Your Start Screen Settings

You can customize the Start screen via its settings. Windows 8 groups a lot of features that used to be spread about the different parts of the Windows user interface into one place: the PC Settings app. To access Start screen settings, access the Settings charm while on the Start screen. The Start screen's Settings panel slides in from the right. Figure 2-1 shows the Settings pane that appears when you summon it from the Start screen.

 In this chapter, you will learn how the Settings charm functions in all contexts. First, I'll highlight the various areas of the Settings charm's panel and discuss the settings at the bottom of the pane. Later chapters will cover the settings specific to the content of the chapter—for example, Chapter 3 will cover the settings shown on the Settings panel when you summon it from the desktop.

Figure 2-1   *The Start screen's Settings panel*

As you can see from the figure, the panel is named Start at the top of the panel because you accessed it from the Start screen. Below that you see two links:

- **Settings**   Click this to choose whether to show administrative tools on the Start screen and to clear personal info from your tiles.

- **Help**   This link brings up the Windows Help interface.

The links shown here will differ depending on where in the Windows interface you are when you summon the Settings panel. The links shown are only on the panel when accessed from the Start screen.

At the bottom of the Settings pane you will see six icons and a link below them; these links are always the same regardless of the context in which you summon it:

- **Network**   In Figure 2-1, the word "Network" isn't evident because I've set up a wireless network and you instead see the name of my network and its strength in bars. Select this icon no matter what it says to access your network settings.

- **Volume**   Select this icon to bring up a slider that allows you to increase or decrease your volume between 0 (no audio) and 100 (full blast).

- **Brightness**   Select this icon to bring up a slider that allows you to increase or decrease your brightness between 0 (darkest) and 100 (brightest).

- **Notifications**   Select this icon to turn off all notifications from Windows.

- **Power**   Selecting this icon allows you to shut down, restart, or put your computer to sleep.

- **Keyboard**   This icon shows you the language that your computer is set to use.

- **Change PC Settings**   This link takes you to the PC Settings app, which includes many more settings for you to configure. See the next section for more information on the PC Settings app.

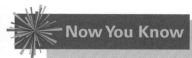

Now You Know **Microsoft Brings Windows in Line with Other Technologies**

Most electronics, including televisions, Blu-ray and DVD players, and so on have a Settings button or something similar that you know to access when you want to configure your device. With Windows 8, Microsoft seems to be bringing Windows into line with other types of electronic devices. Previously, a huge portion of what is now in Settings was in the Windows Control Panel—and it is still there. The difference with Windows 8 is that the most important configuration tools for most users are now also conglomerated under the more intuitive Settings charm for easier access on tablet devices in particular.

Manage PC Settings

You can manage the settings for your Windows 8 device with the PC Settings app, which you can summon by clicking Change PC Settings at the bottom of the Settings pane (see the previous section). The following sections describe the contents of all the settings available in the same order they are listed on the left side of the PC Settings app, as shown in Figure 2-2.

Personalize Your PC

If you want to customize the aesthetics of your Windows 8 environment, some of the settings to do so are here, although a great many more are listed under the display-related settings in the Control Panel.

The Personalize settings are split into three groups, as you can see at the top of the page in Figure 2-2:

- **Lock Screen**   Lock Screen settings allow you to change the picture you see when you log out of Windows or first boot up the computer. You can choose from one of the default pictures or click Browse to choose your own. Here you can also choose

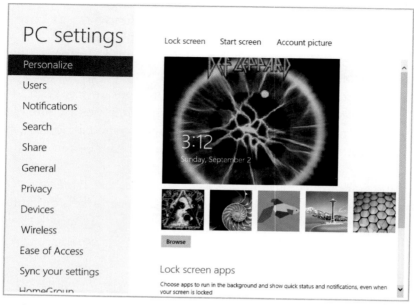

Figure 2-2   *The PC Settings app lets you easily configure your PC.*

which apps are allowed to run in the background even when your computer is locked; alternatively, you can choose to let no applications have this ability.

- **Start Screen**   Click this link at the top of the page to choose from available color configurations for your Start screen and highlight color on certain apps, and also to choose from various available designs for the Start screen background.

 The highlight color is the color you see when on the Start screen or in the PC Settings app. Figure 2-2 shows a blue highlight color.

- **Account Picture**   Unlike previous versions of Windows, Windows 8 allows you to easily make your account picture your own face or whatever other photo you'd like. Click the Browse button to choose an image from your computer or click the Webcam button to snap a shot to use immediately.

Change User Settings

User settings allow you to switch your account from a local account to a Microsoft account (or vice versa), change the way you sign in to your computer, and add users.

 Windows 8 is the first version of Windows to allow users to customize the way they sign into their computers. You can choose to use a four-digit PIN to log in instead of your full password or even choose an image password that allows you to unlock your computer by drawing symbols on an image using a touchscreen interface.

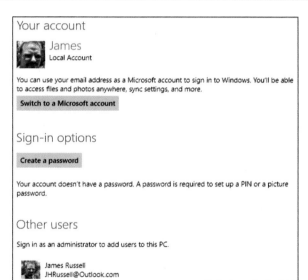

 To delete or modify user accounts, you'll still need to use the Control Panel.

Customize Notifications

Previous versions of Windows notify you about many things in various ways. Many apps notify you via the desktop's system tray, for example.

In Windows 8, use this menu item to either disable or enable app notifications and their sounds. You can also choose to opt in or out of notifications from various applications such as Internet Explorer.

Configure Searches

Windows 8's search functionality goes far beyond that of previous versions of the operating system by letting you search within certain apps, not just searching in files and folders. The settings under this item let you delete your history or toggle certain apps on or off from being searchable. You can also choose whether to allow Windows to personalize your search experience by remembering former search terms for future autocomplete suggestions, as well as put results from the most-searched apps at the top of your results listings.

Set Up Sharing

Windows integrates sharing for the first time from Facebook, LinkedIn, Twitter, and more. Use these settings to customize Windows sharing.

Decide whether to allow Windows to show recent searches, and if so how many, as well as whether you want the most-shared apps near the top of the sharing list when you access it. You can also disable sharing in any of the apps that use it by clicking the switch next to the application's name to toggle its sharing features on or off.

Change General Settings

This group of settings is pretty large, encompassing a wide variety of options. The main items here include

- **Time**   Change your time zone here.

- **App Switching**   Decide whether or not you want to use app switching here and choose to clear your app switching history should you want to.

- **Spelling**   Windows, like Microsoft Word, now includes a spelling and grammar checker throughout its interface. Choose here whether to turn them off or on.

- **Language**   If you use alternate keyboard layouts for other languages, clicking the link in this section will take you to the language settings in the Windows Control Panel. From there you can change your keyboard layout and language.

- **Available Storage**   See how much storage space your PC has available.

- **Refresh Your PC Without Affecting Your Files**   Choosing this option will remove most of your applications, if not all of them, and refresh your PC if it's not working properly without affecting your files.

- **Reset Your PC**   Completely wipe your PC and start over again. Use this option if you want to sell or give away your PC and reset it to its default configuration.

 This will completely erase all of your files, applications, and settings. If at all possible, back up your files before using this option.

- **Advanced Startup** Choose this option if you're having trouble with your computer. You can choose to restart the computer without networking, for example, or access and use System Restore to reset your PC to a time when it worked properly.

Configure Privacy

The Privacy settings include allowing or disallowing Microsoft to use your data to improve its Windows Store and whether to allow your information—including your name, account picture, and location—to be used in applications that other people could potentially see online.

 If you are uncomfortable with any information about you being potentially seen by others, toggle these switches to Off.

Configure Devices

This section displays devices such as printers, an external keyboard and mouse, external monitors, and so forth. Simply click a device to work with its properties or click the Add Device button to add a new device. I discuss devices in more depth in Chapter 13.

Set Up Wireless

If you have any wireless devices available, they will be shown in the right pane here where you can click on each to work with it. You can toggle all wireless devices and switch Airplane mode off and on.

Configure Ease of Access

People who have sensitive sight or other vision conditions can configure their display to suit them. The settings here allow you to choose high-contrast options, increase the size of text and images on the screen, and select Windows narration settings, among others.

Sync Your Windows 8 Settings

Syncing your settings allows you to log in to another Windows 8 computer with the same Microsoft account as your home computer and have your settings from your home computer load right up on the new computer. Your default theme, bookmarks, File Explorer settings, and HomeGroup login settings—among other things—move seamlessly wherever you do.

Manage HomeGroups

A HomeGroup allows you to more easily network the computers you have in your home or office network. These settings allow you to configure which folders you share on your computer and whether media devices such as Xbox 360 can access media files on the computer. This section of the PC Settings app also displays the password needed for other computers to be able to access the HomeGroup.

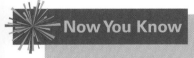

Now You Know **Get a Microsoft Account to Sync Settings Between Computers**

If you used a non-Microsoft account—that is, with an e-mail address that doesn't end in @outlook.com, @live.com, @hotmail.com, or @msn.com—you're not going to be able to use Microsoft's synced desktop settings. If you didn't create a Microsoft account when you first logged in to your machine, you can easily do so via a Web browser and then come back to the PC Settings app to add the Microsoft account to your Windows 8 computer. Microsoft's Outlook .com addresses are by far the best accounts for your purposes; see Chapter 14 for information on getting an Outlook.com account.

Check Windows Update

Check your Windows Update settings every so often to ensure no important updates are available—especially if you have Windows Update configured for manual updating. Click the Check for updates now button and Windows will look to Microsoft's servers to see if any updates for Windows are available. If so, Windows will download and install them. You really can't change any settings from here; you'd need to go into the Control Panel to do so. I discuss updating Windows in more depth in Chapter 5.

Windows Update

You're set to automatically install updates

We'll install 1 important update automatically.
It'll be installed during your PC's scheduled maintenance. This update was found today.
We'll continue to check for newer updates daily.

Check for updates now

3

Control Your
Windows 8 Desktop

The Windows 8 desktop is more versatile than the utility was in previous versions of Windows—by far. As described in Chapters 1 and 2, Microsoft has retrofitted Windows 8 with an interface that works on tablet computers as well as it does on laptops and other PCs.

Functionally, the Windows 8 desktop is the same desktop you've seen for years. The Start button is no longer on the taskbar, but (as discussed in Chapter 1) is easily accessible via corners or edges. You may click 18 times on the Internet Explorer icon mistaking it for the Windows orb at first, but you'll get used to that quickly. In this chapter, I'll teach you how to get used to this latest iteration of the Windows desktop in no time at all.

Remember that the desktop tile is a click, tap, or press away wherever you are in Windows. You can get there by clicking the desktop tile on the Start screen, and as described in Chapter 1 you can get to the Start screen with a single motion and click or a swipe and a tap from anywhere in the Windows interface.

 You can also press the WINDOWS key on a keyboard at any time to summon the Start screen and, if you put the Desktop tile in the very upper left position on the Start screen, you can tap the ENTER key to go from the Start screen to the desktop.

Switch Applications with Task Switcher

The Windows 8 task switcher allows you to multitask in a fashion much like how the Windows taskbar works but with Windows Store apps instead of desktop apps. To access the Windows 8 task switcher, hover your mouse in the upper left corner.

 If you've only just started Windows and nothing happens, you won't have any applications to switch between.

To get used to how the task switcher works, test the feature out:

1. Open two or more Windows 8–style applications from your Start screen.
2. Go back to the desktop and hover your mouse in the upper left corner or swipe from the left edge with your finger. A thumbnail of the other open app(s) appears alongside any other recent apps.
3. Choose to do one of three things as follows:
   - Click or tap an app's thumbnail to return to that app.
   - Click or tap and drag a thumbnail to snap it to the left or right of the desktop.
   - Move below the open thumbnail and click or tap the Start thumbnail at the bottom of the screen.

 Right-click or tap and hold on any item in the task switcher and choose Snap Left or Snap Right to view Windows Store apps on either the left or right side of your desktop.

Change Desktop Settings

The desktop has its own version of the Settings panel just like any other Start screen tile, and it is from here that you can change the desktop settings. Desktop-specific settings are located under the name "Desktop" at the top of the pane, and general settings that are available on all settings pages are at the bottom of the pane.

Unique to the desktop's settings panel are the top four:

- **Control Panel**   Click this link to summon the Control Panel.

- **Personalization**   Click this link to open the Personalization window of the Control Panel, from which you can change your current theme or configure similar settings.

- **PC Info**   This link opens the PC Info section of the Control Panel from which you can give key information about your computer to support personnel. For example, the information tells you exactly what processor you have and how much RAM you have, which can help you in cases where you have to troubleshoot your PC with a support technician over the phone and you need all the critical information about your PC's configuration in one place.

- **Help**   Click here if you want to browse through Microsoft's help documentation.

Configure Startup Applications

Absolutely every program you can think of wants to be in the boot sequence of your computer so it preloads and thus starts faster, but you can configure your startup applications so they don't slow down your Windows boot sequence every time you start your computer.

Here's how to disable startup applications using the Task Manager utility:

- Right-click or press and hold the Start button and choose Task Manager to summon that window. Select the Startup tab, which is shown in Figure 3-1. As you can see, the window tells you the actual impact of the item on the system boot process:

  - **None**   The item doesn't slow your computer's startup process at all.

  - **Low impact**   The item has minimal impact on the startup process.

  - **Medium impact**   The item slows down the process to some degree.

  - **High impact**   The item slows down your PC's startup significantly.

 If a startup item has no major impact on boot, consider just leaving it enabled. Applications do tend to run better when they are part of the boot sequence.

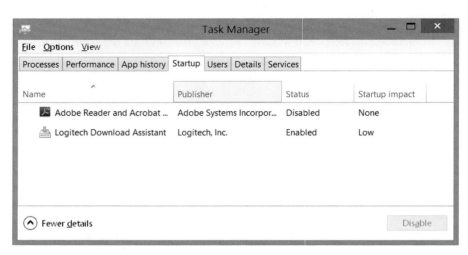

Figure 3-1   *Use the Task Manager to change startup items.*

- Carefully decide which startup applications you want to disable. As you can see in Figure 3-1, I have Adobe Reader in the startup, which is already disabled.

 Know what you're disabling before you disable it. Google the exact name of the application along with a word such as "startup" to find out what the service is exactly.

- Click or tap an item and then click or tap Disable or Enable to perform that action.

Customize the Desktop

Customizing your Windows 8 desktop lets you make it really yours by moving items where you want them, using themes to change desktop backgrounds and colors, and configuring your taskbar the way you want it. The following sections show you how to do these things and more.

Change Your Display Settings

Display settings you can change for Windows 8 include screen resolution, text size, and multiple desktops. The following sections describe how to perform each of these tasks.

Change Screen Resolution

You may want to change your screen resolution for any number of reasons, the main reason being if you're attaching a new monitor to your PC and the default resolution isn't what you want for whatever reason. Here's how:

1. Right-click or press and hold on the desktop itself.

2. Choose Screen Resolution. The Screen Resolution window appears, as shown in Figure 3-2.

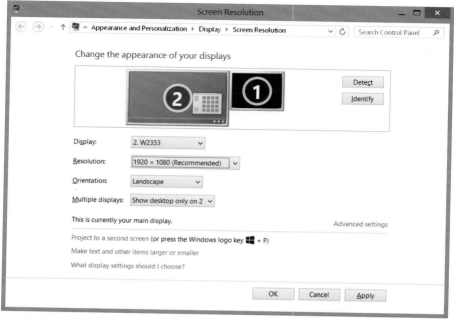

Figure 3-2 *The Screen Resolution window*

3. Choose the desired resolution from the Resolution drop-down menu and click Apply.

4. Windows opens up a box asking you to confirm the change or it automatically reverts back to the previous resolution. If all looks well, click OK.

 One resolution will usually say "Recommended" next to it. This is what Microsoft and your monitor's manufacturer believe to be the best setting for your monitor.

Make Your Monitor's Text Bigger or Smaller

If you have a particularly large or small monitor, you may want to make the text of the Windows interface larger or smaller to compensate. With a monitor set at 1920×1080 resolution, it might be difficult for you to read the text on your screen. Here's how to change the size of text in Windows:

1. Access the Windows Control Panel and select Appearance and Personalization.

2. Select the Make Text or Other Items Larger or Smaller link at the right under the Display heading. The Display window appears, as shown in Figure 3-3.

3. Either choose one of the three options with radio buttons next to them—Smaller (100% Default), Medium (125%), and Larger (150%)—or utilize the drop-down menu and text input box at the bottom of the window that allows you to change the font size for individual interface elements such as title bars, menus, and icons.

4. Click Apply and close the Control Panel.

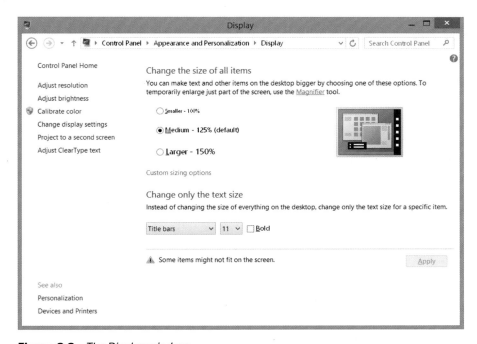

Figure 3-3   *The Display window*

Configure a Second Monitor

Adding a second computer monitor to your PC lets you utilize both screens together to increase the screen real estate you have to work on—if you are adding a larger screen than your original screen, you are more than doubling the amount of space you have to work with. Here's how to configure a second monitor:

1. Plug your second monitor into the computer and install any drivers that came with it if necessary—most modern monitors do not require additional drivers and will work after being plugged in. Restart your computer to ensure Windows fully recognizes it and that it's functioning properly.

2. Access the Windows Control Panel and select Appearance and Personalization.

3. Click or tap Display and then click the Change Display Settings link at left on the Display window that appears. The Screen Resolution window appears, as shown in Figure 3-3.

4. Click or tap the Detect button at the top of the screen. If you're not sure which monitor is which—1 or 2—click or tap the Identify button to display a large number 1 and 2 on each display.

5. Choose one of the following options from the Multiple Displays drop-down menu:

   - **Duplicate Displays** Most useful for presentations or playing media through televisions, this allows you to display what is on your screen on another screen.

   - **Extend Displays** Use both monitors as two sides of basically one desktop. You can have different windows open on each screen and drag windows from one screen to the other.

   - **Show desktop Only on 1** Choose this to not display anything on monitor 2.

   - **Show desktop Only on 2** Select this to display nothing on monitor 1.

6. Click or tap OK and close the Control Panel.

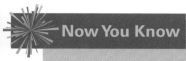

Extended Display Facilitates Multitasking

Say you're studying research on your favorite hobby in your Web browser and you are writing a related report or other document on the subject at the same time. With one screen, unless it's big enough that you have both windows cascaded on the same screen, you have to minimize one app to see the other. With dual screens you can have a research document open on one screen, your document open on the other screen, and then you only need look from screen to screen to see, copy, paste, and so forth between the two. This saves you from continuously minimizing the browser to view the document, minimizing the document to see the browser, and so on.

Transform Your Desktop with Themes

Windows themes are basically a group of color settings for the taskbar and window elements as well as one or more desktop backgrounds that when combined change the look of the Windows desktop pretty dramatically. For example, Figure 3-4 shows the Microsoft Best of Bing theme displaying a spectacular image of mountains.

Windows 7 was the first version of Windows to support the use of dynamic themes that automatically update not only your desktop background but also the color of windows and the taskbar so as to match the colors in the desktop image. New RSS desktop backgrounds periodically download new images by checking in every so often with Microsoft's servers online. The following sections describe how to change your theme, get more themes, and create and save themes for sharing with others.

Change Your Theme

Changing your theme allows you to personalize your desktop's background picture as well as the window and taskbar colors in one

Figure 3-4 *The Microsoft Best of Bing theme*

fell swoop. You can change your theme via the Control Panel easily. Just follow these steps:

1. Right-click or press and hold on the desktop and choose Personalize to summon the Personalization window, as shown in Figure 3-5.

2. Click any theme to switch instantly to that theme. Close the Display window.

 Some themes are not for aesthetics; high-contrast themes were made to help people who have vision difficulties see the different elements of their screen easier.

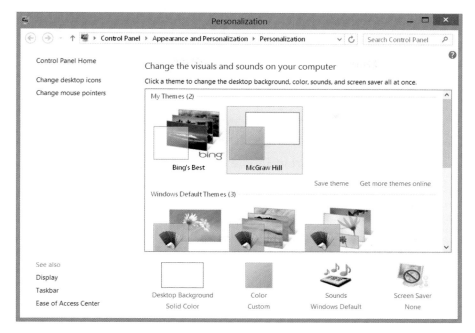

Figure 3-5   *The Personalization window*

Get More Themes Online

Microsoft posts dozens of themes online for different versions of Windows. To find more themes for Windows 8, follow these steps:

1. Right-click or press and hold on the desktop and choose Personalize to summon the Personalize window.

2. Scroll through the themes until you see the Get More Themes Online link. Select it.

3. Microsoft's themes page will open in your Web browser. From this page you can access links at the left of the page to see categories of themes. If you find a theme you like, click the Download link next to it, choose to open the file after it has been downloaded, and the theme will install itself and become the active theme automatically.

Modify and Save a Theme

If you just want to tweak an existing theme a bit and save it for personal use or sharing, here's how:

1. Right-click or press and hold on the desktop and choose Personalize to summon the Personalize window.

2. Choose a theme and modify it using the Sounds, Background, Window/Taskbar Color, and Screen Saver controls on screen.

3. Right-click your current theme and choose either Save Theme or Save Theme for Sharing. Name your theme in the resulting box and click Save.

4. If you chose Save Theme for Sharing, Windows creates a desktop theme package file in your My Documents folder by default. Send that file to someone else who is using Windows 8 and they can install that theme simply by double-clicking or double-tapping the file.

Customize Your Taskbar

Like most things in Windows, you can customize the taskbar significantly. You can move it, make it bigger, add toolbars to it, auto-hide it, and configure and choose the icons displayed on it. The following sections show you how to configure your taskbar to make processes such as accessing open applications, viewing system tray notifications, and starting often-used applications easy.

Customize Your System Tray

Your system tray is the right-most section of the taskbar that shows a few icons—most or all of which are probably white to indicate that they are Windows-related—and the clock. Each of these icons represents an application or utility that is running in the background.

It seems that every application wants to be running in the system tray, and to do so they typically insert themselves in the Windows start sequence. In the following sections, you'll learn how to configure which applications should be in your start sequence and system tray and I'll show you how to make them behave the way you want them to.

 A lot of applications that start in the Windows boot sequence have system tray icons. See the next section to deal with startup applications.

System icons in the system tray are related to your computer's functioning. Some indicate external devices, others indicate antivirus software that is always running, and still others tell you the status of your PC's volume, network strength, and security status. Most of these apps and services are started by the programs themselves, not by you.

Here's how to access these icons and change whether they appear and in what cases they do so:

1. Click the arrow to the left of the system tray and choose Customize. The Notification Area Icons window appears, as shown in Figure 3-6.

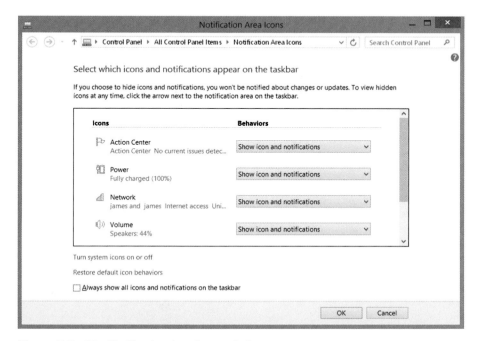

Figure 3-6 *The Notification Area Icons window*

2. From each item in the center pane of the window, choose one of the options from the drop-down list box to determine whether to show or hide the icon and whether notifications from that item will be displayed or not.

3. Click or tap the Turn System Icons On or Off link to summon the System Icons window, as shown in Figure 3-7. From each item in the center pane of the window, choose Off from the drop-down menu to turn that icon off.

 Click or tap the ever-present Restore Default Icon Behaviors link on the page if at any point you want to restore the default system tray icon and notification settings.

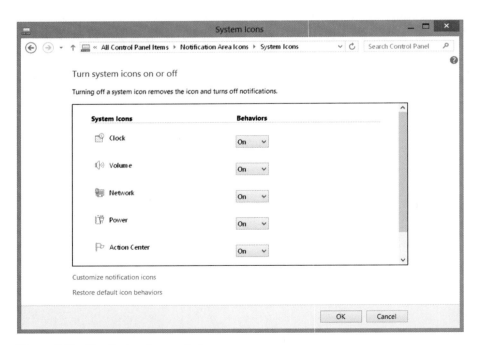

Figure 3-7   *The System Icons window*

Customize Your Taskbar Icons

To change your taskbar icons, simply right-click or press and hold one and then choose Delete to remove it, or right-click or press and hold any tile on the Start screen and choose Pin to Taskbar to add an icon to your taskbar. You can click or tap, drag, and drop any icon on the taskbar itself to move it back and forth.

Add Toolbars to Your Taskbar

By default, Microsoft does not enable everything that can be on the taskbar, likely feeling that the default items reflect most users' preferences. However, different users have different needs, and if you want to add a toolbar to the taskbar, you can. To add a toolbar to your taskbar, simply right-click or press and hold on an empty spot on the taskbar and choose the name of a toolbar to add from the list of the four available. You can add the following toolbars to the taskbar:

- **Address**   This toolbar adds an address bar like you see in a Web browser at the right side of the taskbar. You can simply type in a Web address and press ENTER or tap the arrow icon to the right of the bar to open the link in the desktop version of Internet Explorer.

 If you use another browser as your default browser, this address bar won't respect that choice. It'll open the URL in Internet Explorer anyway.

- **Links**   Add this toolbar to the taskbar if you want to be able to access your Internet Explorer favorites (the links are the same as any links on your Favorites toolbar in Internet Explorer, which is hidden by default).

- **Touch Keyboard**   This toolbar really isn't one. It's an icon that summons the touch keyboard. If you do not have a touchscreen you can use your mouse to interact with the keyboard.

- **Desktop**   These links are on your desktop, or perhaps not. Some of these items are not actually shown on the desktop by default, including the Control Panel, links to your libraries, and more.

- **New Toolbar**   Choose this option to create a toolbar that represents a folder on your hard drive. Items in that folder will appear as items on a list on the new toolbar.

Resize Your Taskbar

If your taskbar isn't big enough to handle everything you want to add to it you may want to make it bigger. Or, if you remove enough items, you may want to make it smaller. You can resize the taskbar easily by performing the following steps:

1. Right-click or press and hold on an empty spot on the taskbar.

2. Remove the checkmark next to Lock the Taskbar if it's there. Locking the taskbar prevents you from making accidental changes to it, which is especially easy with a touchscreen device.

3. Hover your mouse or finger over the top edge of the taskbar and drag your mouse or finger up or down to increase or decrease the size of the taskbar.

4. Repeat Steps 1 and 2 but check the check box in Step 2 instead of removing the checkmark to once again lock the taskbar.

Move Your Taskbar

Moving your taskbar is really easy to do. You can move it to the top, left, or right sides of the screen, or if you've moved it and want to move it back you can easily move it back to the bottom of the screen where it started.

 To see in real time where you want the taskbar if you're not sure, right-click or tap and hold on the taskbar, clear the check box next to Lock the Taskbar if necessary, and then drag the taskbar to the top, bottom, right, or left of the screen and drop it there.

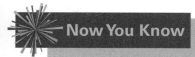

The Old Quick Launch Toolbar Has Been Assimilated

The Quick Launch toolbar, which was a new feature in Windows 98, used to be mostly hidden by default and included small icons such as the Show Desktop button, Windows Media Player, and Internet Explorer. Windows 7 integrated the Quick Launch toolbar into the main taskbar interface and made the icons larger. It also allowed you to add the original Quick Launch toolbar for some bizarre reason, but the original is now gone in Windows 8.

You can also use the Personalize settings in the Control Panel to do so—if you happen to be on the window anyway, for example, this might be easier:

1. Right-click or tap and hold on the desktop itself and choose Personalize to summon the Personalize window.

2. Click the Taskbar link in the lower left corner of the window. The Taskbar window will appear.

3. Choose one of the four sides of the screen in the Taskbar Location On Screen: drop-down menu and click OK.

Hide All Open Windows

You can hide all open windows by clicking or tapping the tiny Show Desktop button at the very right of the taskbar—it hardly looks like a button until you hover over it—and even then it is merely everything to the right of the very thin black line that appears. All open windows will instantly be minimized when you click this button. Hover in the extreme lower right corner of the desktop to use the Peek feature discussed in the next section.

Disable or Enable Peek

Peek, which you can disable or enable at will, is a feature that makes all windows become totally transparent so you can see how many windows you have open. The feature was carried over from Windows 7 but is barely visible in the final version of Windows 8. Access it by hovering your mouse button or finger in the extreme lower right corner of the desktop and taskbar. Here's how to disable or enable Peek:

1. Right-click or tap and hold the desktop and choose Personalize from the menu that appears to bring up the Personalize window.

2. Click Taskbar in the lower left corner of the window to summon the Taskbar Properties window.

3. Add or remove the checkmark from the (extremely long-winded) check box at the bottom of the Taskbar tab labeled Use Peek to Preview the Desktop When You Move Your Mouse to the Show Desktop Button at the End of the Taskbar; then click OK.

Enable or Disable Auto-hide

You can enable or disable the Auto-hide feature. Auto-hide gives you more screen real estate to work with because the taskbar disappears until you sweep your mouse down to the lowest point on the bottom of your screen. Here's how:

1. Right-click or tap and hold the desktop and choose Personalize from the menu that appears to bring up the Personalize window.

2. Click Taskbar in the lower left corner of the window to summon the Taskbar Properties window.

3. Add or remove the checkmark from the Auto-hide the Taskbar option near the top of the Taskbar tab to enable or disable the option as desired and click OK. The taskbar will then disappear; simply move your mouse to the bottom of the screen to summon it.

4

Organize Files with File Explorer

File Explorer—known in previous versions of Windows as Windows Explorer—used to be almost hidden in older versions of the operating system, but it has become known as a key navigation tool and more recent versions of Windows have made it easier to find and access the utility as a result. Windows 8 puts File Explorer where it always belonged: on the desktop's taskbar. Windows 8 has also significantly upgraded File Explorer's user interface, making it an even more indispensable tool for navigating your computer's files, folders, and devices. In this chapter, you'll learn how to use the new File Explorer to organize and manage all of your files as well as how to create and configure library folders.

Access File Explorer

No matter what app you're in or whether you're on the desktop or the Start screen, you can access File Explorer in one of several ways:

- **From the taskbar** File Explorer is by default one of the two icons pinned on the taskbar, right next to Internet Explorer; just click or tap the icon.

- **From the old Start menu** Summon and right-click or press and hold the Start button in the lower left corner of the screen and choose File Explorer.

- **From the All Apps area of the Start screen** Click or tap the File Explorer tile; it's under the Windows System group.
- **Search for it** Search on "File Explorer" using the Search charm and select the File Explorer tile when it appears.

Navigate File Explorer

Open File Explorer and click the white down-pointing arrow in the upper right corner of the window under the Close, Maximize, and Minimize buttons. The ribbon drops down, and as you can see in Figure 4-1 the upper region of the window in particular looks a lot like a Microsoft Office application, not least because of the presence of the ribbon.

The main features of the File Explorer interface are as follows:

- **The Quick Access Toolbar** At the extreme top left corner of the File Explorer window is a toolbar with tiny icons that you can customize, just as you can in Office, by adding features you want constantly accessible to it (see the "Customize File Explorer" section near the end of the chapter for more information).

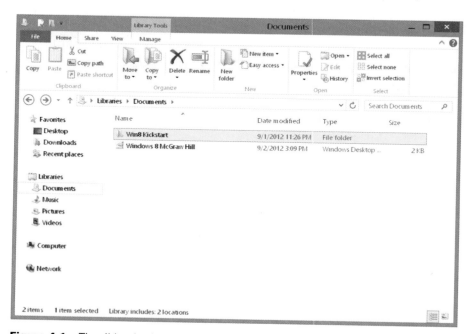

Figure 4-1 *The ribbonized version of File Explorer*

- **The ribbon** Although the ribbon is hidden by default, clicking the down-pointing arrow in the upper right corner of the File Explorer window drops it down for you. Below the Quick Access Toolbar are tabs, the first two of which mirror the first two tabs in any Microsoft Office application, File and Home:

  - **File** This tab is present regardless of where you click or tap in the left pane and contains shortcuts to your most recently viewed folders.

  - **Home** This tab is present on every item except if you select Network and includes the most popular features that people use when working with File Explorer such as Cut, Copy, Move, New Folder, Delete, Rename, and so forth. All of the key file-management tools are here.

  - **Share** This tab is present on nearly all items that you click in the navigation pane and allows you to share files via e-mail, compress files, fax files, and network share.

  - **View** Also present on nearly all items in the navigation pane, this tab allows you to customize the File Explorer view.

  - **Other tabs** Tabs to the right of the aforementioned four will change depending on the folder you're in. See Figure 4-1 for an example of the new ribbonized interface that's visible when you're in the Pictures folder.

- **The Navigation bar** This bar may remind you of a Web browser navigation bar. At left you'll see a Back button (it lights up only when you have a location to go back to), a blue arrow Up button that takes you up a folder from the current one, and across the center near the top of the window you will see the address bar that shows your current folder path.

 Click or tap on any single item in the folder path in the address bar to go to that folder. You can also drag and drop items onto a folder item in the address bar to move them to that folder.

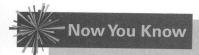

Now You Know — Office's Ribbon Is Now in File Explorer

Office 2007 introduced a very different look for the Office interface, and presented the *ribbon*. The ribbon does away with drop-down menus at the top of the screen and replaces menus with tabs that display groups of related functions such as icons, drop-down menus, and buttons. With Windows 7, Microsoft brought the ribbon to non-Office applications such as Paint and WordPad. With Windows 8, Microsoft has brought the ribbon to bear on the entire File Explorer interface itself, and the result is a much more contextually aware, smarter, and more intuitive File Explorer interface.

- **The Navigation pane** The pane in the left side of the File Explorer window is where you can select an item to see its contents in the larger right pane. You can also use the arrows next to each item to open it in this pane and drill down into each item that way.

- **The Preview pane** The pane at the right side of the window shows items selected in the Navigation pane in more detail. Different folders behave in different ways in this pane. For example, if you're looking at images in the Pictures folder, you'll see large images in the preview pane, whereas if you are looking at files in the Documents folder, you'll see previews of the actual documents in the pane.

Choose How to View Files

Before you really dig in and start working with your files, it's good to know how to customize how you view them first. File Explorer contains a slew of view options. The View tab has four main sections, each of which gives you successively more granular control over your view than the one before it. The following sections discuss each pane from left to right.

Change Pane Options

Change your pane options to suit the way you want to work with File Explorer. The following options are available to change your pane options:

- **Navigation Pane**   All major settings related to the left-most Navigation Pane are here. Click the button to drop down a mini pane where you can choose to show all folders, favorite folders, expanded folder structures showing the path to the current folder, or none of these options. You can also uncheck the Navigation Pane option at the top of the mini pane to remove the navigation pane altogether.

- **Preview Pane and Details Pane**   These options are mutually exclusive. You can choose one or the other or neither but not both. If you choose neither, you won't see another pane next to your main one. If you choose the Preview Pane, every image you select will be previewed in as close to real size as File Explorer can fit it (depending on the size of your window) in a pane to the right of your main one. Choose Details Pane and the image's details will be shown instead.

Change the Layout of Icons

The default layout of your icons may not suit you, but rest assured you can customize the layout easily. Each library view by default is customized for the file types that it is named after—for example, the Pictures library is customized for images, and so the default view is for large icons. Select the View tab on File Explorer to see the following layout options:

- **Extra Large Icons** As the name states, these icons are huge. Each folder is displayed as open with two of the pictures (or folders if there are less than two pictures) within it appearing in thumbnail form "inside" the folder. Figure 4-2 shows extra large icons in 1024×768 resolution.

- **Large Icons** Just as with Extra Large Icons, each folder is displayed as open with two of the pictures (or folders if there are less than two pictures) within it appearing in thumbnail form inside the folder. These icons are about half the size of those in the Extra Large Icons view and about twice the size of the Medium Icons view.

- **Medium Icons** As with the previous two views, each folder is displayed as open with two of the pictures (or folders if there are less than two pictures) within it appearing in thumbnail form inside the folder. These icons are about half the size of those in the Large Icons view and about twice the size as the Small Icons view.

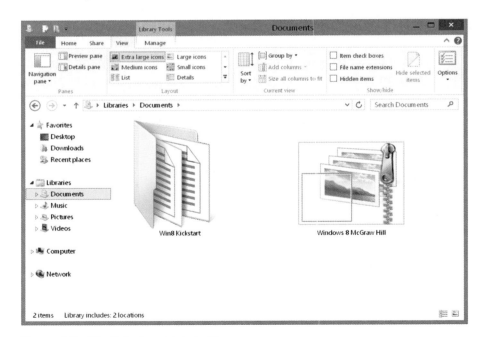

Figure 4-2   *The Extra Large Icons view*

- **Small Icons** This view displays only small folder icons with nothing else shown. You simply see small folders and their names.

- **List** The List view looks much like the Small Icons view, at least in terms of the size of the icons and the information displayed, but in this view the icons are arranged in a descending list format instead of displaying across the top of the pane as they do in the Small Icons view.

- **Details** This view looks like the List view but includes multiple columns across the pane, showing details such as date created, tags, size, and rating.

- **Tiles** The Tiles view shows icons about the same size as those in Medium Icons view, although the tiles also display information about each folder or file, including the type of file (or just "File Folder" for folders) and the size of the image.

- **Content** This view includes the smallest image thumbnails (smaller than in Medium Icon view) and simply lists the name of each file or folder and its thumbnail image.

Tweak Your Current View

The Current View section of the File Explorer View tab allows you to further tweak your view settings. There are four buttons present. The main two apply to any view, and the lower right two buttons (the last two in the following list) apply only to the Details view and will be grayed out in all other views:

- **Sort By** Choose an item in the list that drops down when you click or tap this button to sort items in your current view by various criteria, including by name, date, and other options.

 Both, this item and Group By have an option to choose Ascending or Descending format. Descending will list from top to bottom and Ascending lists from bottom to top. So, if you have items listed by name, files that start with "A" will come before files that start with "Z" in Ascending format; the reverse is true with Descending.

- **Group By**   Group items in your current view in the list that drops down when you click or tap this button to sort items in your current view by various criteria such as name, date, and other options. The difference between this and the Sort By option is that the items will appear in groups together if you use this feature.

- **Add Columns**   Click or tap this button to add additional columns to Details view.

- **Size All Columns to Fit**   Click or tap this button to make columns in Details view fit better on screen.

Fine-Tune Your View with Other Options

The last named section on the File Explorer View tab is the Show/Hide section, and this is where you can fine-tune your File Explorer view. Click or tap to clear or check boxes to show file extensions, check boxes

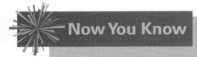

Now You Know   **Lesser-Seen Tabs on Items in the Navigation Pane**

Selecting non-library items in the navigation pane will often bring up tabs not seen elsewhere:

1. Click or tap any drive under the Computer item in the navigation pane to see a Drive Tools box with a Manage tab underneath it. Select this tab to work with your drive.

2. Select the Computer item to see a Computer tab that houses options for uninstalling programs, mapping a network drive, opening the Control Panel, viewing System Properties, and more.

3. Select the Network item in the navigation pane and you'll see a Network tab that includes options for networking, including connecting to a remote computer, opening the Network and Sharing center, or adding devices and printers.

on items to enable easier copying/pasting/moving, or show hidden items. Select a file and click or tap the Hide Selected Items button to hide any images you don't want shown in the folder view.

 If you enable check boxes on file and folder icons, you no longer need to hold CTRL down to select multiple files.

View Advanced Options

The right-most section on the View tab is unnamed and houses only the Options button. With this you can further customize your views of files and folders. See the "Configure Advanced Options" section near the end of the chapter for more information.

Manage Your Files

Your PC is all about the files and programs on it that let you work with and manage those files, and File Explorer is your key tool for doing so. The following sections show you how to upload, view, file, or get information about your files.

Upload Files from an External Device

Uploading your files to your PC from an external device is a different process depending on the device or media that you're uploading from. Some devices come with their own software—printers with print software, for example—in which case you have to learn to use that software on your own. Some of the steps to upload files are the same regardless of the device, especially if you're not using a device's software to do so:

1. Connect your camera or other device such as a smartphone or flash drive to your PC. Chapter 13 describes how.

2. Find the external device in the navigation pane of File Explorer (or by browsing to it manually if you've hidden the navigation pane) and click or tap on it. The device opens as a folder, as shown in Figure 4-3.

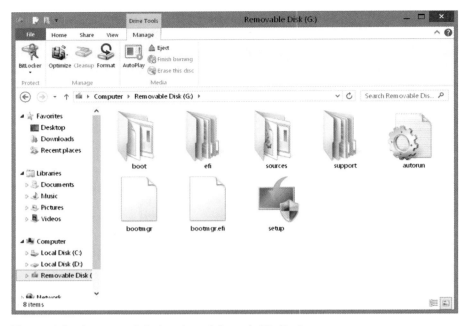

Figure 4-3 *An external device viewed through File Explorer*

3. Browse the device's folder structure until you have copied files you want to copy to the PC to your clipboard by pressing CTRL-C.

 If you want to remove the files from the device, press CTRL-X to cut the files instead of copy them.

4. Use File Explorer to browse to the location on your PC (such as your Pictures library) where you want to copy the files to, click or tap in the appropriate pane, and then press CTRL-V to paste copies of the file in that location.

Organize Files

To organize your files, create folders by clicking or tapping the New Folder button on the File Explorer Home tab to help manage your files.

You can use as many subfolders as you like. For example, you might choose to have folders named after years in the main Pictures library view and then under each year folder include a folder for each outing or event. For example, the "2011" folder might include "Miami Trip," "Grand Canyon," or "Mike's Birthday" folders.

Share Files

Microsoft has taken Windows 8 into the realm of sharing via social media, and the File Explorer Share tab is prime evidence.

As you can see, the Share tab has two main sections:

- **Send** From this section, you can choose to e-mail, zip (compress), burn to disc, print, or fax your images by selecting one and clicking or tapping the appropriate button.

- **Share With** This section allows you to create or join a HomeGroup, share a photo with a specific person, or stop sharing a file altogether.

- **The third, unnamed section** This houses only the Advanced Security item with which you can view and audit permissions. Permissions are an advanced administrative topic that's outside the scope of this book.

Permissions are critical, no matter what app you use, especially if you have sensitive information being potentially shared on a HomeGroup or PC you share with others.

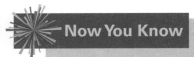

Give Others Access to Your Files

If you choose a library in the navigation pane of File Explorer and then click or tap the arrow next to it, you will see two folders that will differ depending on which library you're in. For example, if you're in the Pictures library, you'll see My Pictures and Public Pictures; if you're in the Videos library, you'll see My Videos and Public Videos; and so forth. Any files that you put in a Public folder such as Public Music will be accessible to others who have an account on your PC or users in your HomeGroup. You can also share files with others using the Share tab while in a library.

Manage Library Folders

Library folders are not actual folders, but are each rather a customized view of one or more folders on the hard drive. The four core libraries are really a combination view of two (by default) folders that contain documents, pictures or other images, videos, or music. Libraries that you create yourself are extremely customizable and give you the ability to create unique views of the files on your hard drive.

Before library folders, the only way you could really view the combined contents of two folders was to make copies of the files in both folders and then paste all of those files into one folder. A library folder allows you to create a customized view of two or more folders that appears to combine the contents of both folders without actually doing so. Fewer copies of files on your hard drive means more space for other files.

Get to Know the Core Four Library Folders

Windows 8 carries over the same four library folders from Windows 7: Documents, Music, Pictures, and Videos. Each folder is optimized for the type of files it is meant to house; Documents doesn't use Large Icons view, for example, but Pictures does because picture icons are visual and document icons are not. Each of the core four libraries is a top-down view of two folders: the Pictures library includes My Pictures and Public Pictures folders, the Videos library includes My Videos and Public Videos folders, and so on.

Just as you'll find in Microsoft Office, in Windows 8 some tabs only appear when you're in certain folders and when present are highlighted by colored boxes in the title bar of the File Explorer window. For example, if you click or tap the Pictures folder, you will see a lavender "Library" box with a yellow "Pictures" box to the right of it. Both have a Manage tab underneath to imply you use them to "manage" your pictures library or pictures with them, respectively. Similarly, if you're in the Music folder, you'll see a "Library" box next to a yellow "Music" box with a Play tab underneath it; selecting this tab shows you options related to playing your music. In this way, File Explorer offers you the tools you need depending on the folder you're in, giving you context-sensitive control over your files and folders.

 Hover your mouse cursor over a file's icon in any library to view information about it. For example, if you hover over a video file in the Videos folder, you'll see its type, size, and length. There is no equivalent for touchscreens, unfortunately.

Your "My" and "Public" library folders for your core four libraries folder may seem at first glance like they have no part of the structure of the main (usually C:) drive on your PC. The address bar, while in the My Pictures folder, for example, says "Libraries > Pictures > My Pictures," but this isn't the exact location of the folder. A "library" is actually just a view of multiple folders on the C: drive. Do the following to see where the folders actually are:

1. Open File Explorer and select the library in the navigation pane.

2. Click or tap the arrow next to the library's item and you will see two folders.

3. Right-click or press and hold on the "My" folder (My Pictures, for example) and choose Properties. The location is shown as C:\Users*Your_User_Name*, so the path for the My Pictures library is actually C:\Users*Your_User_Name*\Pictures.

4. Right-click or press and hold on the "Public" folder (such as Public Pictures) and choose Properties. The location is shown as C:\Users\Public, so the full path for the Public Pictures folder is C:\Users\Public\Pictures.

View Documents

The Documents library used the Details view by default because you're more likely to want to view details about documents rather than view large icons of them—especially given that document icons all look the same. Depending on the type of documents—Microsoft Word and other Office files work well—you can even preview or read the entire document in the preview pane. The Documents library by default includes file-related columns, including Name, Date Modified, Type, and Size. Figure 4-4 shows File Explorer previewing a Word document, specifically the Word document that eventually became this chapter.

While in the Documents library you will see a Library Tools box with a Manage tab underneath it in addition to the four standard tabs that

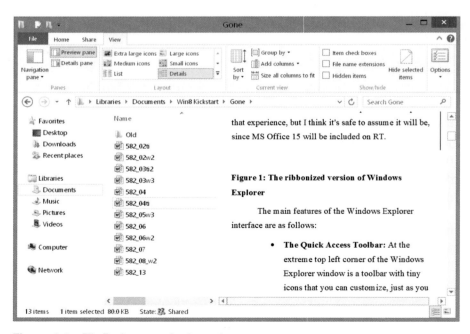

Figure 4-4   *File Explorer previewing a document*

I discussed earlier in the chapter. The Manage tab's ribbon includes two sections: one is called Manage and the other is unnamed. Use the tools in the Manage section to add or remove folders to the Documents library using the Manage button, change the save location for the library, restore default settings, or change other options such as whether to show the Documents folder in the navigation pane.

Manage Pictures

Photographs and images are important parts of many people's personal and work lives, and Microsoft has made Windows 8 the most photo-friendly version of Windows yet. You can customize the Windows 8 Pictures folder via its ribbon interface. You will see two boxes with Manage tabs underneath them in addition to the four standard tabs that I discussed earlier in the chapter:

- **Library Tools** This tab's ribbon includes two sections: one is called Manage and the other is unnamed. Use the tools in the Manage section to add or remove folders to the Pictures library using the Manage button, change the save location for your folders, restore default settings, or change other options such as whether to show the Pictures folder in the navigation pane.

- **Picture Tools** Items related specifically to photographs are on this tab. You can click or tap to start a slide show, rotate an image, set an image as your background image, or even play a slideshow on another device.

Play Music

Playing music is easy in Windows 8 (it's discussed in Chapter 10 extensively). In this section, I discuss the particulars of the Music folder and using the Details view with columns displayed by default, such as Title, Artist, # (as in song number), Contributing Artists, and Album.

Select the Music folder. In addition to the four standard tabs that I discussed earlier in the chapter, you will see two boxes: the first with a Manage tab underneath it and the second with a Play tab underneath it.

- **Library Tools** This tab's ribbon includes two sections: one is called Manage and the other is unnamed. Use the tools in the Manage section to add or remove folders to the Music library using the Manage button, change the save location for the library, restore default settings, or change other options such as whether to show the Music folder in the navigation pane.

- **Music Tools** This tab houses items related specifically to music. You can use these tools to play music, work with playlists, or play music on another device.

Watch Videos

Viewing and watching videos in the Videos folder is easy: the folder uses the Large Icons view so you can visually tell one video from another. Each movie file has its own large thumbnail. In addition to the four standard tabs that I discussed earlier in the chapter, you will see two boxes: the first with a Manage tab underneath it and the second with a Play tab underneath it:

- **Library Tools** This tab's ribbon includes two sections: one is called Manage and the other is unnamed. Use the tools in the Manage section to add or remove folders to the Videos library using the Manage button, change the save location for the library, restore default settings, or change other options such as whether to show the Videos folder in the navigation pane.

- **Video Tools**   Items related specifically to videos are on this tab. You can use these tools to play videos, work with playlists, or play a video on another device.

Configure Library Folders

Library folders are highly customizable in Windows 8. You can change the location of where files are saved and add or remove folders to or from the Library view. The following sections show you how to customize the location or add or remove folders.

Change a Library's Save Location

Changing a library's save location works the same in any library. Here's how to change the save location for either the My Documents or Public Documents folders, for example:

1. Open File Explorer and select Documents in the navigation pane.

2. Select the Library Tools tab and click or tap the arrow on the Set Save Location button to drop down a menu.

3. Choose either "My" or "Public" folder (such as My Documents or Public Documents) and then click or tap to choose the folder you want to change the save the location to. When you drop down the Set Save Location menu again, you'll see that the folder you chose last has replaced the previous location.

Add Folders to a Library

If you have files in other locations on your computer besides within the main library folders (My Pictures and Public Pictures, for example), you can add a folder to your main library so that the folder will be viewable from the main library in File Explorer. Here's how, using the Pictures library as an example:

1. Open File Explorer and select Pictures in the navigation pane.

2. Select the Library Tools tab and click or tap the Manage Library button to summon the Pictures Library Locations window, as shown in Figure 4-5.

3. Click or tap the Add button, browse to and choose the folder you want included in the Pictures library, and then click or tap on the Include Folder button. Then click OK.

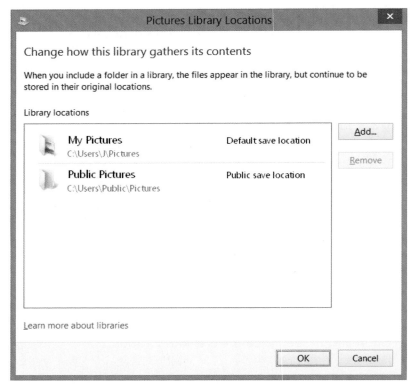

Figure 4-5   *The Pictures Library Locations window*

Remove Folders from a Library

You can easily remove a folder within a main library folder that you no longer want displayed. Just perform the following steps:

1. Open File Explorer and select the library you want to remove in the navigation pane.

2. Select the Library Tools tab and click or tap the Manage Library button to summon the Library Locations window.

3. Choose the folder you want to remove and then click or tap the Remove button. Then click OK.

Create a Library

The core four libraries can only be customized so much. If you want to really customize libraries, you can create your own. Here's how:

1. In File Explorer, right-click or press and hold on the Libraries item in the navigation pane, choose New, and then Library.

2. Right-click or press and hold on the new library in the navigation pane and choose Rename. Type in a name for the new library and then click or tap OK. You cannot designate a save location until you add at least two folders to a library; the button will be grayed out on the ribbon for a newly created library with only a single folder. The Restore Settings button is grayed out as well because user-created libraries have no default Microsoft settings to restore to.

3. Select the Manage tab under the lavender Library Tools box at the top of the window, and then click or tap the Manage Library button. The Library Locations window appears for your new library, as shown in Figure 4-6.

4. Click or tap the Add button, browse to and then select a folder you want to include in the new library. Afterward, click or tap the Include Folder button. Repeat for as many folders as you want to add to the library.

5. Select the Optimize Library For drop-down list and choose from General Items, Documents, Music, Pictures, or Videos.

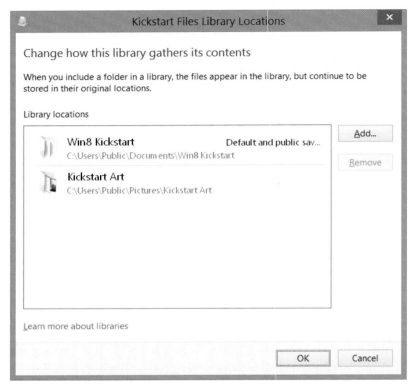

Figure 4-6 *The Library Locations window*

6. Select the "Show in Navigation Pane" item to toggle the option on or off depending on whether or not you want the library to appear in the File Explorer navigation pane.

 If you choose not to show a library in the navigation pane, you'll have to click or tap to drop down the Libraries item in the navigation pane to access that library.

7. Select the Change Icon option if you want to change the library's icon. Either choose one of Microsoft's default icons or click or tap Browse and find your own. Icon files must have the .ico extension.

Customize File Explorer

File Explorer is customizable even beyond changing your view, working with libraries, and other tasks discussed earlier in the chapter. In addition to customizing the Quick Access toolbar and other toolbars, you can configure File Explorer options using the Options button on any View tab.

Customize the Quick Access Toolbar

Originally found in the Microsoft Office suite, the Quick Access toolbar is a very useful new addition to the Windows 8 version of File Explorer. Here's how to add or remove buttons to it:

1. Click or tap the arrow at the very right of the Quick Access toolbar and choose Customize Quick Access Toolbar.

2. Choose an item so that it has a check box next to it to add it to the Quick Access toolbar or clear the check box to remove an item from the toolbar. You can choose from the following actions to add: Undo, Redo, Delete, Properties, New Folder, and Rename.

3. Choose Show Below the Ribbon if you want the Quick Access toolbar below the ribbon.

 The icons go onto the toolbar in the order that you select them. If you don't like the order they are in, just deselect them and reselect them in a different order.

Configure Advanced Options

To customize advanced options for viewing and working with your files and folders using File Explorer, select the View tab, click or tap the Options button, and then choose Change Folder and Search Options. The Folder Options dialog box appears, as shown in Figure 4-7 where the View tab is shown (the General tab appears by default).

The Folder Options window has three tabs:

- **General** Choose here from options showing the very basics of how File Explorer works. Here you can choose to have new windows launch when you click or tap items instead of the pane simply changing to the new folder, as was standard behavior in

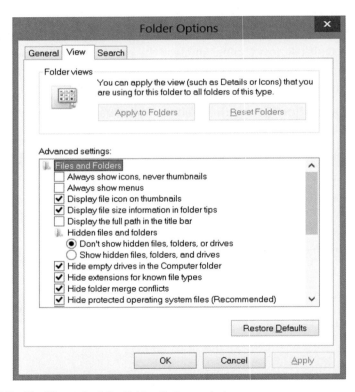

Figure 4-7 *The View tab of the Folder Options window*

Windows 3.*x*—as well as whether to allow single-clicking or single-tapping on links below files and folders to open them instead of requiring double-clicking or double-tapping, and you can choose from options to customize which folders appear in the File Explorer navigation pane.

- **View**   This tab includes extremely granular controls over what you see in File Explorer and in what context. The options on this window are too numerous and varied to include in this book, but as you can see from Figure 4-7, you can choose from all sorts of options, including the popular option to show hidden files and folders in File Explorer.

- **Search**   From this tab, you can customize the way Windows searches your computer. For instance, you can choose to force Windows to always search not only the file names but also the content of documents, which would take significantly longer than a regular search but allows you to search within documents from Windows search.

You Can't Customize the Ribbon

You would expect that, as in Office, you would be able to add or remove buttons from the ribbon in File Explorer, but sadly it isn't so. The Minimize the Ribbon item on the Customize the Quick Launch Toolbar menu—in addition to the little arrow in the upper right below the Minimize, Maximize, and Close buttons—represent the only customization you can perform on the ribbon. You can choose to show it or hide it, but there's nothing else you can do to it.

Get Help with File Explorer

If you need additional help using File Explorer, click or tap the Help icon in the upper right of the File Explorer menu below the Minimize, Maximize, and Close buttons, and next to the Maximize/Minimize the Ribbon arrow button. The Windows Help and Support window, shown in Figure 4-8, appears with what Windows predicts you want help with depending on where you are in the File Explorer interface when you click or tap the button. You can also search on keywords in the Search field.

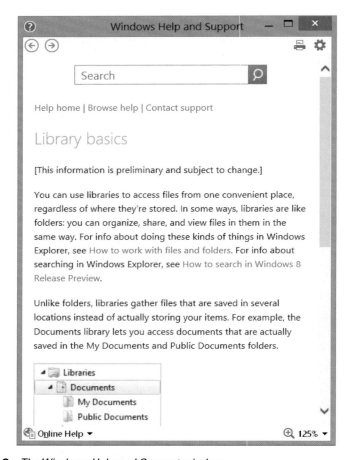

Figure 4-8   *The Windows Help and Support window*

5

Keep Windows 8 Up to Date and Secure

Windows 8 contains advanced update and security features far beyond what previous versions of Windows had, including Web filtering to protect you from malicious Web sites and fairly robust parental controls. In this chapter, you'll learn how to update Windows 8 and protect it from malicious software and hackers.

Manage Security with the Windows 8 Action Center

You can manage security and updates via the Windows 8 Action Center, which is accessible via the little flag icon that sits in your System Tray that notifies you if a security-related issue arises on your computer.

 Although there are very few things you can do in the PC Settings app in terms of security, you can still add users and change passwords and even password types—such as a four-digit PIN or a picture password to which you can assign multiple finger gestures to unlock. The PC Settings app is discussed in Chapter 2.

Here's how to configure the Windows Action Center:

1. Click or tap the flag icon in your System Tray to see your computer's current status.

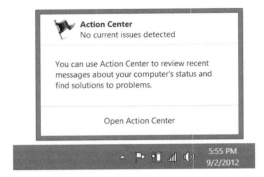

2. Select Open Action Center. The Action Center window appears. If Windows detects any issues with your PC, those problems will be listed at the top of the window in the right pane. If no issues exist, the window looks like it does in Figure 5-1.

3. Click or tap the down arrow to the right of the Security heading in the right pane. You'll see a list of security software and its status on the right.

4. Select the down arrow to the right of the Maintenance heading in the right pane. The top item, for example, is the Check For Solutions To Problem Reports item, which displays whether the feature is on. If it is, Windows will automatically check for solutions to program crashes, operating system glitches, and so on. You can click the Settings link to change the feature or turn it off.

5. Click or tap Change Action Center Settings in the left pane near the top of the window to summon the Change Action Center Settings window. Uncheck all notifications you do not want to see in either the Security Messages or Maintenance Messages sections. Select OK.

 If you have problems that you don't see listed in the Action Center, you can select the Troubleshooting or Recovery links to try those options.

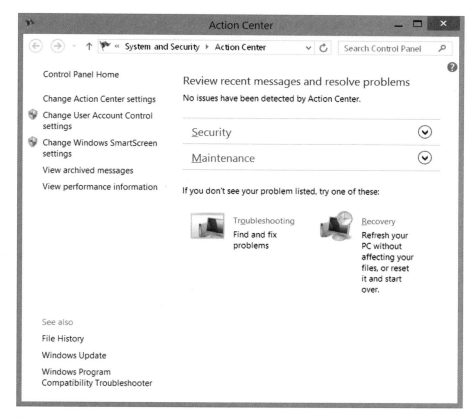

Figure 5-1   *The Windows 8 Action Center*

Updates should not be considered optional if your computer or other device is Internet-enabled. Viruses, Trojans, and other malware are real, and no matter how careful you are, chances are you will run across someone trying to give you malware in some fashion.

 People find new ways to hack into and exploit Windows all the time, and Microsoft periodically closes those holes with ongoing security updates for its currently supported operating systems. If you don't update your computer, your operating system still has those holes and can be exploited.

Note that Windows is not alone in needing security updates—it's just the biggest target. Even Android and OS X are susceptible to viruses, but with around 90 percent of the world's computers running Windows, hackers get the most bang for their buck by creating malware targeting Windows.

To properly secure a PC, antivirus software and a firewall are key, but they're not enough. Antimalware software is better at searching for adware and spyware than antivirus software is, and so you should have at least one program for that as well. If you use native Windows software, you could get away with just Windows Defender and Windows Firewall, since Defender is antimalware software that has been upgraded with significant antivirus capabilities for Windows 8.

Configure Security Software

Installing and configuring security software such as antivirus software, a firewall, and spyware and other malware scanners is a critical part of keeping your computer and personal information safe and private. The following sections show you how to set up the native Windows 8 security software and how to find other software should you wish to.

 If your computer came with security software suites other than what is described here, see your computer's documentation or look online to research the product and find out how to set up and configure it.

Set Up Windows Defender

Set up Windows Defender to help keep your computer safe from spyware and viruses. Windows 8 adds more antivirus features to Windows Defender than previous versions of Windows, making it equivalent in scope to Microsoft Security Essentials, which is a downloadable antivirus suite for previous versions of Windows.

1. Open Windows Defender by right-clicking or pressing and holding a blank part of the Start screen, and choosing All Apps, and then selecting Windows Defender under the Windows System section. Windows Defender appears.

2. Select the Settings tab. The Home tab is shown in Figure 5-2.

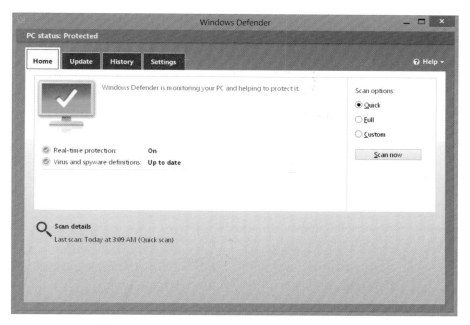

Figure 5-2   *Windows Defender's Home tab*

3. Choose any of the items at the left side of the screen to customize the following settings:

- **Real-Time Protection**   Leave this item checked to have your computer alert you to problems. Uncheck it if you want to manually check Windows Defender for problems.

- **Excluded Files and Locations**   You can select Browse, choose a file or folder, and then click or tap Add to remove files or locations from Defender's scan.

- **Excluded File Types**   Type in file extensions that you want Defender to ignore. Separate multiple items with a semicolon.

- **Excluded Processes**   You can click Browse, choose a file or folder, and then click Add to remove processes from Defender's scan.

- **Advanced**   These advanced options allow you to disable or enable scanning of archived files or removable drives, whether to create a system restore point before trying to fix problems, whether to allow other users of the computer to see full scan history results, and how long to wait until quarantined files are automatically removed.

- **MAPS**   The Microsoft Active Protection Service connects your computer to Microsoft's to allow the company to be notified of malware problems on your computer so they can continue to update Windows Defender and make it as useful a utility as possible.

 MAPS can help improve your computer's security because Microsoft has more information about your computer that it can use to protect your computer with.

- **Administrator**   A single check box here enables Windows Defender or disables it if you uncheck the box.

4. Select the History tab to see any previously quarantined or allowed files.

5. Choose the Update tab to see when Defender was last updated. You can click the Update button to attempt to update Defender immediately.

6. Click or tap the Home tab to view the computer's status and to choose to scan immediately. You have the option to perform a quick, full, or custom scan.

7. Close Windows Defender when you're done.

Set Up Windows Firewall

Set up Windows Firewall to defend your network from outside hacking and infiltration of outside traffic.

 Windows Firewall is pretty basic. If you're really concerned about security, you should consider turning Windows Firewall off and installing a more robust solution.

Here's how to configure Windows Firewall:

1. Open the Control Panel and click or tap the System and Security link and then Windows Firewall.

2. Select the down-pointing arrow next to either the Private Network item or the Guest or Public Networks item to see information about your current network. An item will say "Connected" next to it if it's a connected network.

3. Choose a link at left to configure Windows Firewall. Below the Control Panel Home link, which just takes you back to the main Control Panel window, are the following Windows Firewall–related links:

   - **Allow an App or Feature Through Windows Firewall**   Choose this link to summon the Allowed Apps window, as shown in Figure 5-3. Here you can select which apps are allowed to communicate through the Windows Firewall. Click Change Settings to manage apps settings, Remove to remove an app or feature, or Allow Another App to choose from a list of apps to allow through Windows Firewall.

   - **Change Notification Settings**   Select this link to turn Windows Firewall on or off, block all incoming connections on public or private networks, and select whether or not Windows notifies you when it blocks a new app.

   - **Turn Windows Firewall On or Off**   This link leads to the same window that the link above it does. Choose the appropriate options to turn Windows Firewall on or off.

   - **Restore Defaults**   Selecting this link summons a window with a single Restore Defaults button you can press to reset Windows Firewall to its default state.

Pressing the Restore Defaults button will erase any customizations you've done to Windows Firewall.

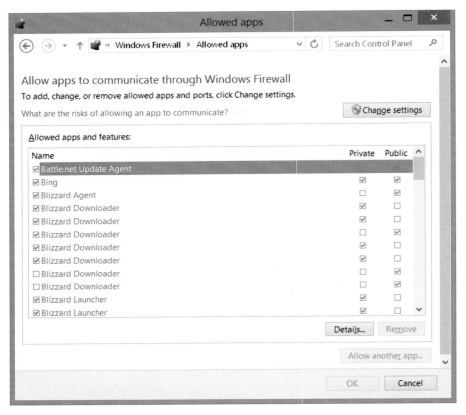

Figure 5-3 *The Allowed Apps window*

- **Advanced Settings**   Choose this link to configure advanced firewall settings such as rules, profiles, and policies.
- **Troubleshoot My Network**   Selecting this link summons a general network troubleshooting utility.
4. Click or tap OK after making changes, if necessary, and close the Control Panel.

 Letting an app through Windows Firewall is something you should consider carefully, especially on public networks where your transmitted information can be more easily compromised.

You will have to balance the risks of allowing the app through the firewall with not being able to use the program. Notice in Figure 5-3 that a number of Blizzard entries are listed. These listings are for *World of Warcraft*, which is made by Blizzard Entertainment. *World of Warcraft* simply won't work properly without being allowed through the firewall. Blizzard knows the security risks and has authenticators that spit out random numeric codes when you are logging in with your password that you can use for additional security, as do similar games like *Star Wars: The Old Republic*.

Find Other Security Software

Security software is a huge industry, and both Microsoft and other companies have created some great security software for you to choose from. The following sections describe other Microsoft security software available for your Windows 8 device and a few top non-Microsoft options.

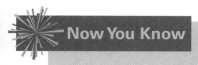
Now You Know

You Don't Have to Use Microsoft's Security Software, But Use *Something*

Microsoft very likely started putting Windows Firewall, Windows Defender, and Windows Security Essentials together not because it necessarily wanted to be part of the security software industry, but rather because most PC users don't bother to set up these features and were simply running their PCs without any security software—and unsecure Windows PCs make Microsoft look bad. So, Microsoft built basic—at first they were *really* basic—security features into Windows XP Service Pack 2 and later versions of Windows to basically force users to use *something* by default. Although Microsoft's security software does get high ratings, it still doesn't hurt to try out other security software. In some cases, you might have to, because some viruses and malware can hide from some security suites but not others.

Find More Microsoft Security Tools

Microsoft does have a few more security tools available, but really there are two key free options for you in addition to the other software described elsewhere in this chapter:

- **BitLocker Encryption** Available in the Control Panel under the System and Security group, BitLocker Encryption allows you to encrypt files on a particular hard drive to make it more difficult for hackers to be able to access key information such as your password.

- **Windows Security Essentials** Available online, Windows Security Essentials is an antivirus suite that is more for folks on Windows 7 or earlier because Windows Defender in Windows 8 has been upgraded in its antivirus capabilities to be roughly equivalent in power and scope to Windows Security Essentials.

Find Non-Microsoft Security Tools

Microsoft security software is adequate, but if you want to find more advanced security software, you have quite the selection to choose from. Some of the more popular security software includes:

- **Avast! Free AntiVirus** Avast! offers free and paid versions of its antivirus software and has a great reputation for solid antivirus protection, ease of use, and compatibility with other products. Available from Avast.com, the company claims 150 million users, which they say is more than any other antivirus software.

- **AVG Free AntiVirus** AVG Free is a highly rated free antivirus suite that also offers paid versions. AVG also has protection for mobile devices and is available from free.avg.com.

 Using a paid version of software usually gives you more protection than free versions, especially for commercial use.

- **Comodo Firewall** Comodo Firewall is a free product, but you can also pay for antivirus capabilities if you want to go with a single firewall and antivirus solution. Comodo Firewall is available from personalfirewall.comodo.com.

- **Malwarebytes Anti-Malware**   This package is available from Malwarebytes.org and touts fast scan speeds, the ability to use its "Chameleon" feature to be unblocked from malware that has hidden from it, and cooperation with other security software.

 If you choose to go with non-Microsoft security software such as a configuration including Avast! AntiVirus, and Comodo Firewall, you need to turn off Windows Defender and Windows Firewall before installing the new software because you should not have two firewalls or two antivirus programs running simultaneously. They will conflict with each other and possibly affect your computer's performance in some negative fashion. That said, if you decide to go back to Windows Defender and Windows Firewall, uninstall the previous security suites, restart your computer, and then turn Defender and Windows Firewall back on.

Update Windows 8

Windows update has been streamlined significantly during the course of the last decade and a half as new releases of Windows have come about, and Windows 8 is no exception. Updating Windows has never been as seamless and simple as it is in Windows 8, and the operating system allows you unprecedented choices regarding how much control you want over updates. Some users, for example, may prefer to view and approve each individual update, while others may not want to be bothered with the matter at all and would rather set Windows to update itself without user intervention. In the following sections, I'll show you how to update Windows whether you want to have complete control—or none whatsoever—over the process.

Access Windows Update via the PC Settings App

Windows Update used to be accessible via the All Programs menu on the Windows Start menu, but this is no longer the case. The Windows Update feature is now available via the PC Settings app and from the

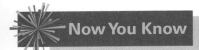

Now You Know · Windows Updates Have Improved Dramatically

With Windows XP Service Pack 2 in particular, Microsoft in the last decade has had some egg on its face in terms of updates. That service pack, in many cases, could not be installed successfully on various computers and actually rendered other users' computers inoperable. This is why Microsoft lets you uninstall Windows updates if they do not play well with your computer. However, since Windows Vista and Windows 7, Windows Updates have a much better track record of *not* harming or rendering useless users' computers, so even if you've had issues with Windows Updates in the past, you might want to give Microsoft another chance and see if you don't have a better experience with Windows 8.

Control Panel. The PC Settings app is much easier to use but is less functional than the Control Panel interface.

Here's how to access Windows Update via the PC Settings app:

1. Access the Charms bar and click or tap the Settings charm.

2. Select Change PC Settings at the bottom of the Settings pane.

3. Choose Windows Update from the options on the left. Windows Update will appear, as shown in Figure 5-4.

4. Click or tap Check For Updates to view any new updates. As you can see from the figure, Windows displays the last time it checked for updates as well as new updates or the time it last installed updates.

Access Windows Update via the Control Panel

The PC Settings app is a great way to update Windows quickly and find out when updates will be installed. But if you want to configure Windows Update in any way, you need to use the Windows Update settings in the Control Panel. To do so, access the Control Panel and

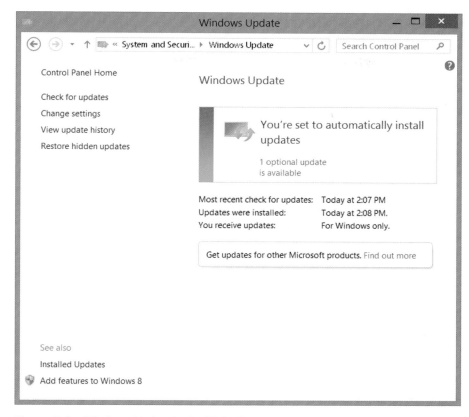

Figure 5-4   *Windows Update in the PC Settings app*

select System and Security. Then select Windows Update. From here you can see on the right pane roughly the same information you see in the PC Settings app, although optional updates are also shown and the dates that updates were installed are also visible, as shown in Figure 5-5.

The key difference between the PC Settings app and the Control Panel is the list of options in the left pane. These options are as follows:

- **Control Panel Home**   Click this link to return to the main Control Panel screen.

- **Check for Updates**   This link will make Windows check for updates immediately.

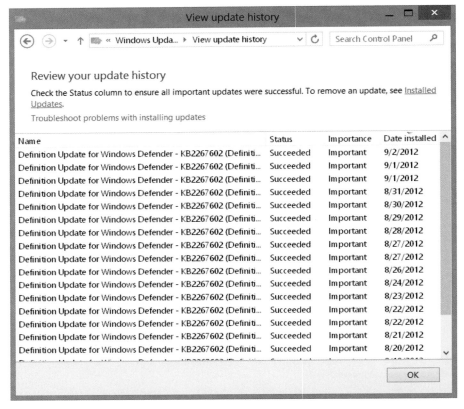

Figure 5-5 *Windows Update history in the Control Panel*

- **Change Settings** Click this link to change Windows Update settings. See the next section for more information on which settings you can change and how.

- **View Update History** If you want to view your update history, click this link. Every update ever installed is listed here along with the status of the update (e.g., whether it successfully installed or not), as shown in Figure 5-5. Click the Installed Updates link at the top of the window to remove installed updates, as shown in Figure 5-6.

- **Restore Hidden Updates** If you've previously hidden any updates that you either did not want to install or could not install, you can restore them to the list of updates by clicking this link.

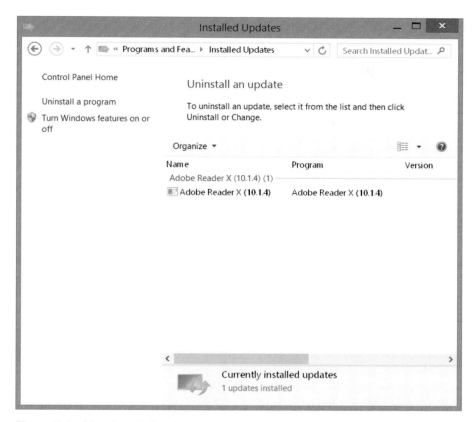

Figure 5-6   *View installed updates.*

- **Installed Updates**   To remove any installed updates, click this link to view currently installed updates. As shown in Figure 5-7, you'll see updates broken down in a list according to whether they're updates for Windows or another application and you will be able to click each and then click Uninstall to remove them.

 Some items may have a Change button in addition to an Uninstall button so you can configure the update instead of just uninstalling it if you wish.

- **Add Features to Windows 8**   If you want to upgrade your version of Windows, click this link.

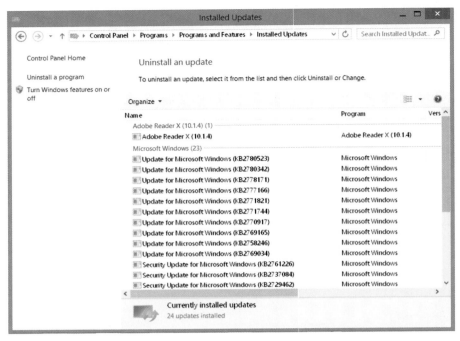

Figure 5-7 *Change or remove installed updates.*

Change Windows Update Settings

Depending on your preferences, you may decide at some point that your current settings allow you too much or too little control over your updates and want to adjust these settings. Here's how to access and change the settings for Windows Update:

1. Access the Control Panel, select System and Security, and then choose Windows Update.

2. Click or tap Change Settings in the left panel to summon the Change Settings window, as shown in Figure 5-8.

3. Change any of the following options as desired:

   - **Install important Windows updates automatically**   Drop down the menu under the Important Updates heading to choose whether to allow Windows to install important Windows updates, such as security updates, automatically.

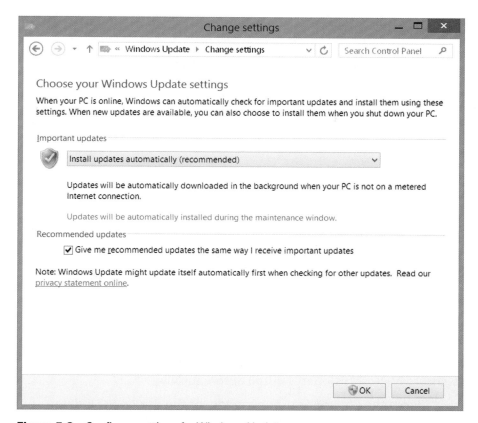

Figure 5-8   *Configure settings for Windows Update.*

Alternatively, you can choose to have Windows download updates but notify you before installing them, notify you before downloading them, or not look for updates at all.

 Windows updates increase the security of your system significantly. Choose to have Windows not search for updates at your own risk.

- **Apply Important Updates settings to optional updates**   Check this check box if you want to apply the settings described in the preceding bullet to optional updates.

- **Apply Important Updates settings to updates to Microsoft Update** This option allows Windows to update other Microsoft products, such as Microsoft Office, alongside Windows by running Microsoft Update.

 As with Windows, updating Office helps keeps your PC secure.

Update Office Automatically

Versions of Office have had updates and even service packs released for them just like Windows. In Windows 8, updating Office is as seamless a process as updating Windows. Microsoft updates Office via a different service than Windows Update. It's called Microsoft Update, but you'll never need to know the difference between the two if you configure Windows Update correctly. Otherwise, you'll have to review and approve other Microsoft updates, including those for Office and other Microsoft software, alongside their Windows counterparts. Here's how to ensure Microsoft Updates install automatically:

1. From the Change Settings window of the Windows Update section of the Control Panel (see the previous list to see how to get there), choose Install Updates Automatically (Recommended) from the drop-down list in the Important Updates section in the right panel.

2. Check the Give Me Updates For Other Microsoft Products When I Update Windows check box in the Microsoft Update section if it isn't checked already.

3. Click OK.

Configure User Account Controls (UAC)

Configure User Access Controls to customize when or if Windows notifies you about your applications' attempts to make changes to your computer. The feature is useful and can be set up by doing the following:

1. Click or tap on the flag icon in your System Tray and then select Open Action Center. The Action Center window appears.

2. Select the Change User Account Control Settings link near the top of the left pane. The User Account Control Settings window appears, as shown in Figure 5-9.

3. Choose your desired setting by moving the slider and then click or tap OK. There are four settings, the top item being Always Notify (about everything) and the bottom being Don't Notify (at all, ever). The second option down is the default, which only notifies you when applications try to change your PC, and the third option down is identical except that it will not dim your desktop.

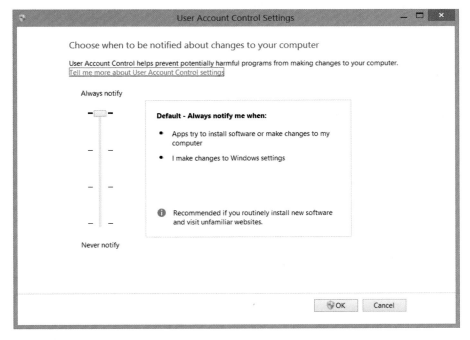

Figure 5-9   *The User Account Control Settings window*

Set and Configure Parental Controls and Web Filtering

Windows 8 allows you to configure parental controls and Web filtering options to restrict computer usage for family members to help keep content they view on the Internet age-appropriate with the new Windows 8 Family Safety Control Panel section. Here's how:

1. Access the Control Panel and select the Set Up Family Safety For Any User link under the User Accounts and Family Safety section.

2. Choose a user to configure Family Safety for and the User Settings window appears, as shown in Figure 5-10. If you need to set up a user, click the Create A New User Account link to do so and then choose that user when you get back to the User Settings window. You can view the current settings for the user on the right side of the right pane.

 Click View Activity Reports to see the user's most recent usage report.

3. Enable Family Safety with the On, Enforce Current Settings radio button in the upper left portion of the right pane.

4. Choose a radio button in the Activity Reporting section to indicate whether you want to collect activity reports about the user's computer usage.

5. Under the Windows Settings section, you'll see the following options, which you can configure as you wish:

   • **Web Filtering**   Select this to choose a Web restriction level for the user. The most restrictive option allows the user to only see Web sites you specifically allow. The least restrictive setting simply warns the user if the browser suspects they are accessing adult content. You can also check the Block File Downloads box if you don't want the user downloading files at all.

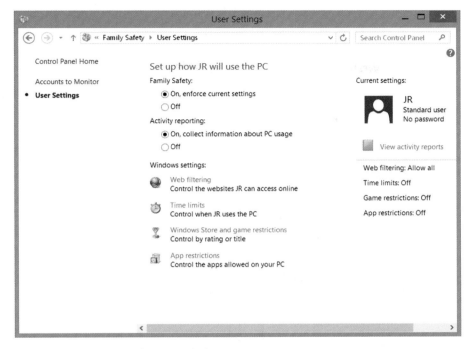

Figure 5-10   *The User Settings window*

- **Time Limits**   Select this link to set a time limit in hours that the user can use the PC per day, or to set a curfew for specific time ranges during the day that the user can use the PC.

- **Game and Windows Store Restrictions**   Selecting this link allows you to configure which games and Windows Store apps the user can use. You can choose a specific rating as a threshold or block specific games or apps.

 You can choose your rating system from the main Family Safety window (the screen before you choose a user to configure in Step 2) by clicking the Rating System link at left.

Part II
Explore Tiles, Media, and Apps

6

Get Started with Windows Store Apps

The Windows 8–style interface comes with a slew of new apps that cover the basics of what PC users need. Later chapters in this part discuss some of these apps that are important enough for their own chapters, such as Music and Video, Games, and Windows Store—and you can skip to those chapters if you like—but in this chapter I get you up to speed with the rest of the default Microsoft apps.

Windows Store Apps 101

To bring Windows 8 to touchscreen tablets, Microsoft created a new interface for working with Windows known as *Windows Store apps*. These apps remind you more of smartphone apps in the way they behave because smartphones have touchscreens and a lot of the same concepts apply to tablets, such as apps taking up the entire screen with no desktop visible. Chapter 1 discusses the basics of working with the Windows 8–style interface, but before I describe specific Windows Store apps I'll give you some of the more intermediate concepts that apply to all of them and focus on each app in particular in later sections of the chapter.

Keep these things in mind as you read through this chapter and other chapters in this part:

- There are usually options available to you that you don't see right away. Right-click or press and hold on something to get a contextual overlay with additional buttons and options.

Alternatively, for a touchscreen interface, swipe down or up—or both—from the top and bottom edges of the screen toward the center to access this overlay.

- It can be easy to get lost in some of these apps at first, so always keep your eye out for a Back button (left-facing arrow) to help you get back to the main screen. If there isn't a Back button, access the context overlay (as described in the first bullet) and see if there isn't a Home button. You can also use the Start charm to get back to the Start screen.

- Access the Settings charm to view and work with any options or settings for that app. Options will vary per app, even depending on where you are in an app. As mentioned in Chapter 11, for example, if you're in a game of "Solitaire" you'll get different options than if you are on the main game screen.

- You can pin many things from within these apps to the Start screen. For example, in the Sports app you can right-click or tap while viewing your team's news page and choose Pin to Start to add a tile featuring news about that team to the Start screen.

Now You Know **You Can Always Find Apps in the Windows Store**

All of the basic apps can be uninstalled and reinstalled via the Windows Store and all default Microsoft apps are there. If you see an app discussed in this book but find that it isn't on your Start screen, do this:

1. Look under All Apps, which can be accessed by right-clicking or pressing and holding on a blank part of the Start screen and selecting All Apps.

2. If it's not there, go to the Windows Store and download and install it from there.

Set Up Mail and Check Messages

Mail is a basic e-mail application with a simple, clean interface (see Figure 6-1) that is designed with three vertical panes instead of the typical setup for e-mail applications with one vertical pane at left and two horizontal panes at right.

 If your screen is at too small of a resolution—as in the figure—the middle pane isn't visible. You will have to click or tap the inbox to view it and click the Back button to move back to the folders view.

Here's how to set up your mail and check messages:

1. Open the Mail app from the Start screen.

2. Access the Settings charm and click or tap Accounts.

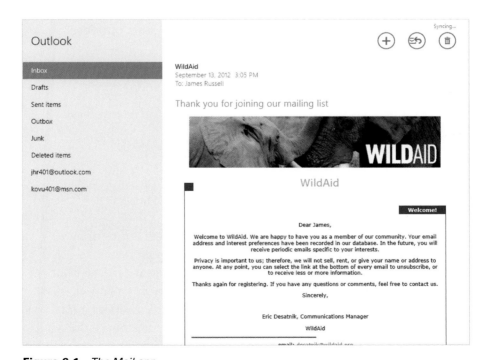

Figure 6-1   *The Mail app*

3. Select Add an Account and choose an account type. You can choose from Hotmail, Outlook.com, Office 365, Google, Yahoo! Mail, AOL, or another account type.

4. Type in your e-mail and password. Your account loads into Mail.

5. Click Inbox in the upper left to check your mail. It will be listed in the center pane. If you have multiple e-mails in a thread, you will see the top e-mail or SMS message and underneath that a line at the left and a later message to the right of the line in lighter gray text. This is called the "conversation view."

6. Click a message in the center pane to see it displayed in the right pane.

7. Choose from one of the buttons in the upper right to interact with the message or create a new one. From left to right they are New Message (the plus symbol), Respond (a picture of an envelope with an arrow), and Delete (a trash can).

8. Right-click or press and hold on a message to see the Sync, Pin to Start, Move, and Mark Unread options. Right-click or press and hold on a folder to see the Sync and Pin to Start options.

 If someone sends you an invitation via Mail, you can choose to accept or reject it from the e-mail itself. If you accept it, it will be added to your Calendar app (discussed in the next section).

 **Now You Know** ## Mail Has Relatively Basic Functionality

Mail integrates well with the Windows 8 interface, but so does Outlook 2013, and if you have that app you probably want to use it or another e-mail client for professional communication. The Mail app is decent for a free e-mail app, but it is pretty basic and at least in its original version doesn't include features such as filters, reply confirmation, or out-of-office notifications. Outlook.com is also a great free alternative. I discuss Outlook.com in Chapter 14.

View and Manage Events with Calendar

Calendar is another very simple-to-use app that allows you to keep track of important dates and events. You can add multiple accounts to Calendar, such as a Google Calendar and an Outlook.com calendar, so you can see and interact with both under a single interface. Here's how to add an account to Calendar and set up an event with it:

1. Open the Calendar app from the Start screen, access the Settings charm, and click or tap Accounts.

2. Select Add an Account and choose an account type. You can choose from Hotmail, Outlook 2013, or Outlook.com, or Google.

3. Type in your e-mail and password. Your account loads into Calendar, as shown in Figure 6-2.

4. Repeat steps 1 through 3 for any other accounts you want to add.

5. Access the Settings charm and select Options. From here you can hide individual calendars or change the color in which a calendar's events are listed.

October 2012

Sunday	Monday	Tuesday	Wednesday	Thursday	Friday	Saturday
30	1	2	3	4	5	6
7	8 Columbus Day	9	10	11	12	13
14	15	16	17	18	19	20
21	22	23	24	25	26	27
28	29	30	31 Halloween	1	2	3

Figure 6-2   *The Calendar app*

6. Return to the Calendar screen when finished and right-click or swipe down or up from the top or bottom edge of the screen to summon the Calendar options. You can choose to view one day only, by month, by week, jump straight to today, or create a new event.

7. Select New to create a new event.

8. Type in a title for the event and then a message below it, if desired.

9. Select the date, start time, and event duration in the left pane. Type in a location and choose a calendar to save the event to if you have multiple calendars.

10. Select the See More link at the bottom of the left pane to see more options, such as whether the event recurs, the time for a reminder, what your status will show while you're at the event, to invite other people, or to mark the event private.

11. Click or tap the Save this Event button in the upper right corner (it looks like a floppy disk) to save the event.

 If you add Facebook to the People app (see Chapter 8), Windows automatically populates your calendar with birthdays from your Facebook contacts.

Check the Weather

Microsoft has partnered with Weather Decision Technologies to provide weather data for the Bing Weather app, with which you can check your forecast, see weather maps, and even check historical weather data for your area. Here's how:

1. Open the Weather app from the Start screen. The first time you open it, the app will ask you if it can use your location. Select Allow and the app will load up your local weather, as shown in Figure 6-3.

GROVER BEACH, CA
BING WEATHER

66°

Sunny (Clear)

Feels Like 67°
AccuWeather

MON 17	TUE 18	WED 19	THU 20	FRI 21
66°/50°	65°/51°	68°/55°	68°/50°	68°/5
Partly Cloudy	Partly Cloudy	Partly Cloudy	Partly Cloudy	Partly Clo
2% ♦	1% ♦	0% ♦	0% ♦	1% ♦

Page last updated Monday, September 17, 2012 6:35:26 PM

Figure 6-3   *The Bing Weather app*

2. From left to right you'll see the current weather, your hourly forecast, weather maps, historical weather data, and an advertisement. You'll see tiny arrows in the current weather section just to the left of the Hourly Forecast section that you can select to scroll through your forecast information.

3. Scroll vertically through the Hourly Forecast if it doesn't all fit on your screen, select a map to view a brief video of a weather map, and view either temperature or rainfall in historical weather by selecting the appropriate button beneath that chart. You'll also see a small minus symbol in the lower right corner of the screen. Select it to see the categories all together. Select a category to then go back to the main app screen.

4. Access the Settings charm and choose Options if you want to turn your search history off or on or clear weather searches.

5. Right-click or press and hold to summon the app options. From here you can choose to view weather for different places around the world. You can also change the temperature to Celsius or Fahrenheit or refresh the current weather. Choose Places to add a location.

6. Select the black box with the plus symbol in it and enter a city name. A list of options comes up. Choose the correct option and then click Add.

7. Right-click or press and hold on the new place and you'll see options to pin it to the Start screen. This can be useful if you are traveling and need to keep track of weather in multiple places, for example. You'll also see options to set that place as the default, remove it, or add another place.

8. Right-click or press and hold on the screen and choose World Weather to view a map of the world with temperatures shown alternating between two cities per each of six continents.

Stay Up to the Minute on the Latest News

Microsoft has partnered with a large number of news sources to craft its News app. The News app includes a newspaper-style mix of news called Bing Daily and a customizable My News section that you can use to get news on the topics you want. Here's how to use the News app:

1. Open the News app from the Start screen. Bing Daily appears by default, as shown in Figure 6-4.

2. Click the icon of the "i" in a circle on the top story to see a summary of the story. Click instead on the title to read that story. Click or tap the Back button to return to the main page.

3. Scroll or swipe to the right to view stories in different categories. Click or tap on any category name to see stories in that category or click or tap on any story to read that story.

BING DAILY
TOP STORY

ANALYSIS: OBAMA, ROMNEY
USING CHINA TO SCORE POINTS

AP ASSOCIATED PRESS 3 HOURS AGO

Beyond politics, there are real policy differences that could have a
dramatic impact on the ties between the U.S. and the country that's
the largest foreign holder of U.S. Treasury debt.

Figure 6-4 *The News app*

4. Right-click or press and hold and tap My News from the options
   bar at the top of the screen to go to your My News page.

5. Tap the gray box with the plus symbol in it to add a section. Enter
   a news topic, choose from the list of auto-complete suggestions,
   and click or tap Add to add a section. Add as many sections as
   you like. You can also right-click or tap and hold on this screen
   and choose Add a Section instead.

6. Right-click or press and hold and select Sources if you want to
   see the various sources from which Microsoft pulls news.

7. Access the Settings charm and choose Options to choose another
   language or location; for example, you could choose United
   Kingdom – English if you wanted to view UK news. You can also
   clear your history.

Store It in the Cloud with SkyDrive

SkyDrive allows you to store up to 7GB of files in "the cloud," which is a term for file storage via the Internet that allows you to access files from anywhere in the world you can get an Internet connection. In the case of SkyDrive, your files are stored on Microsoft's servers. Your SkyDrive account is attached to your Microsoft account and can be accessed via iOS, Android, and Windows 8 devices, including Windows RT and Windows 8 Phone. Here's how to set up and use your SkyDrive on Windows 8:

1. Open the SkyDrive app from the Start screen. If this is the first time you've accessed the app, you'll have to sign in with your Microsoft account and watch a tutorial. The SkyDrive app appears showing your folders and/or files.

2. Select the arrow next to your name to switch between viewing your SkyDrive, recent documents, or shared documents.

3. Click or tap on a file to open it in its default program.

4. Click or tap on a folder to open its contents on your screen.

5. Right-click or swipe up from the bottom edge of the screen to access the options for SkyDrive. You can choose to refresh, add a new folder, upload more files, toggle between viewing details or thumbnails, or select everything in the current folder.

6. Access the Settings charm and choose Options to view your SkyDrive storage and how much you've used of it or to check your storage or Recycle Bin via your default Windows 8–style browser.

 SkyDrive is a prominent folder in the left pane of File Explorer. You can also access your files through it.

Search with Bing

Bing is Microsoft's search engine that competes directly with Google. With Windows 8, Microsoft has brought Bing to bear on Windows in a big way, especially with its name. Several of the app tiles on the Start screen fall under the Bing banner, even though their tiles don't belie that fact. For example, the Weather app is actually Bing Weather, the Maps app is Bing Maps when you open it, and so forth. The Bing app, though, is the actual search engine and comes with daily photography just like Bing.com does. Here's the basics of how to use Bing:

1. Start the Bing app from the Start screen and it appears as shown in Figure 6-5. If you're signed into Bing, you'll see a little medallion with a number next to it to the right of the search bar. This is the number of Bing Rewards you have earned.

2. Touch or click one of the four squares that appear over the image to learn four different facts about the image that give you clues to what it is. Each fact comes with an orange link that you can click to find more information on that subject.

3. Click the little icon of an "i" in a circle in the lower left of the image to find out what the image actually is if you couldn't guess from the four facts.

Figure 6-5 *The Bing app*

4. Notice the trending subjects in the lower left of the screen. Click one to search that topic.

5. Select the More button in the lower right corner of the screen to see more trending topics. Click the Back button to get back to the main screen.

6. Click or tap into the text field in the upper left of the screen and start typing a search query. The picture will dim out as you click or tap into the field and popular topics will appear below the text field. You can click or tap any of these boxes to search on that word. As soon as you start typing, the popular searches are replaced with auto-complete suggestions.

7. Access the Settings charm and click SafeSearch to change whether you want Bing to filter out adult content from your searches.

8. Access the Settings charm and click Accounts to sign in to Facebook, Bing, or learn more about Bing Rewards.

9. Access the Settings charm and click Search History to choose whether to keep your search history or to clear your search history immediately.

Get Directions with Bing Maps

Like Google, Bing has a mapping feature. With Windows 8, Bing brings maps and turn-by-turn driving directions to your PC with the Maps app, although this first incarnation of the app does not include walking or transit directions. Here's how to use Bing Maps to get driving directions:

1. Open the Maps app from the Start screen. The first time you do so, the app will ask permission to use your location. Select Allow to use the app. Bing zooms in on your current location.

2. Right-click or press and hold on the screen to access options for showing traffic, changing the map style, returning to your location, or getting directions. Choose Directions.

3. Type in starting and ending locations in the appropriate fields on the pane that appears. The icon with two arrows next to the top field and the little target icon allow you to swap location A for B and vice versa. The little

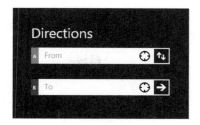

X icon that appears when you type into either field allows you to delete the location.

4. Tap the right-pointing arrow icon next to the bottom field to get directions. Directions from Grover Beach, California, to Redmond, Washington are shown in Figure 6-6.

5. Use the plus or minus buttons to zoom in or out. You can scroll left or right on the directions at the top of the screen to view earlier or later directions. If you zoom all the way in, you can see Microsoft's bird's-eye view showing satellite imagery of the location.

Figure 6-6 *Turn-by-turn driving directions*

Make Travel Plans

In partnership with Frommer's guides and Kayak.com, the Bing Travel app allows you to research travel destinations, including hotels and searching for flights. Here's how to use the Travel app to research a destination, search for a hotel, view information about hotels, and search for flights:

1. Open the Travel app from the Start screen. A featured destination appears at left, and to the right of it you'll see sections for featured destinations, panorama images, and magazine articles. You can click the title of the Featured Destinations section to view more, or click the little "i" in the circle for a summary of the location.

2. Click the Feature Locations title and you'll see various destinations. You can use the Region drop-down at the top left of the screen to focus on a specific region of the world.

3. From anywhere in the app, right-click or press and hold on the screen and choose Destinations to view featured destinations. Choose a destination to open a page for it with various information and photos as well as links to hotels and the ability to search for flights. Scroll to the right and you can see sections for attractions, hotels, and restaurants. At the extreme right you'll see Frommer's content about that destination.

4. From anywhere in the app, right-click or press and choose Flights. Type in information about your intended flight and click Search Flights to view flight information. You can use the drop-down menus at the top of the screen to sort by price, airline, return time, departure time, and number of stops.

5. From anywhere in the app, right-click or press and hold and choose Hotels to search for hotels. Type information about your intended stay into the appropriate fields and select Search Hotels to bring up a list of hotels in your intended destination. You can use the drop-down lists at the top of the screen to sort by price, hotel class, or amenities.

6. From anywhere in the app, right-click or press and hold and choose Best of the Web to view much more travel information. Click or tap any tile on this screen to view the information in your default browser.

Track Money with Finance

In partnership with Morningstar Inc. and Informa Research Services Inc., Microsoft has created a financial application for Windows 8 to allow you to do research on stocks and financial news from one place. Here's how to use the Bing Finance app:

1. Start the Finance app from the Start screen. The app appears with a featured financial article for the day at left. You can select the article's title to read it or click or tap the icon with the "i" in the circle to view a summary of it.

2. Scroll to the right and you see an Indices section showing you the DOW, S&P 500, NASDAQ, and Russell 2000 indices, all of which you can view by day, week, month, or the past year. Scroll further right to see sections for financial news; a stock watchlist; market movers; information on market commodities; rates for mortgages, savings, and credits cards; and fund picks.

3. Right-click or press and hold on the screen and choose from the following sections at the top of the page:

   - **Today** This is the home page you've already seen in previous steps.

   - **Watchlist** The stock Watchlist.

   - **News** This section shows more financial news articles than the Today section.

   - **Rates** View more rates here than on the Today section.

   - **Currencies** View the current values of the world's major currencies.

   - **World Markets** See the current levels of the world's markets on one screen.

   - **Best of the Web** View articles on all sorts of financial topics here; click or tap on an article to summon it in your default browser.

4. Access the Settings charm and select About to view the extensive list of partners Microsoft is working with to bring you the information in this app.

5. Access the Settings charm and click Options to choose another language and location.

Get Sports News and Info

Microsoft has partnered with quite a few organizations, most notably STATS LLC, to bring you the Bing Sports app, with which you can see the latest schedules, scores, sports news, popular players, and popular teams. The Sports app is one of the more customizable of the Windows Store apps. Here's how to get the latest sports information from Bing Sports:

1. Open the Sports app from the Start screen. The app appears with a featured sports article for the day at left. You can select the article's title to read it or click or tap the icon with the "i" in the circle to view a summary of it.

2. Scroll to the right and you see sections for news, schedules, favorite teams, and magazine articles. Click or tap the white box with a plus symbol on it under Favorite Teams to add a favorite team. Select a team here to view a page full of information about them, as shown for the Oakland Athletics in Figure 6-7.

3. Right-click or press and hold on the screen to summon the options. By default you will see a lot of sports in the bar at the top.

4. Select All Sports, click or tap any sport, and choose either Add or Remove depending on whether you are or aren't interested in that sport.

5. Right-click or press and hold on the screen and choose a sport at the top of the page. The page for that sport appears with sections and information customized to that sport.

6. Right-click or press and hold on a sport page and select Glossary to get up to speed fast on the abbreviations and lexicon for that sport. You can also choose Refresh to refresh results immediately.

OAKLAND ATHLETICS
TOP STORY

OAKLAND ATHLETICS

Rank in AL West 2   Record 84-62   Home 44-31   Away 40-31

Figure 6-7 *The Bing Sports app showing right fielder Josh Reddick of the Oakland A's*

7. Right-click or press and hold on the screen and choose Best of the Web to view much more sports news and information. Click or tap any tile on this screen to view the information in your default browser.

8. Access the Settings charm and click Options to choose another language and location, whether or not to auto-refresh the app's data, and if so at what interval.

Shoot Photos and Video with Camera

The Camera app in Windows 8 doesn't have a lot of features to it, but it works just fine to snap photos or take video using your PC's camera. Here's how to take photos or video with the Camera app:

1. Start the Camera app from the Start screen. The first time you start the app it will ask you for permission to use your Webcam and microphone. Select Allow to be able to use the Camera app.

2. Click or tap the screen to take a photo. You will see a three-second countdown appear, giving you time to perfect your smile. Then the picture will snap. You can right-click or press and hold on the screen and select timer to turn this timer off so that your photos and videos will be taken immediately.

Photos and videos that you take will be accessible in your Pictures library both in File Explorer and in the Photos app under the Camera Roll folder.

3. Select the arrow at left after you've taken a photo to view it.

4. Right-click or press and hold on a photo to access Crop and Delete options. For a video, you'll instead see Trim and Delete options. To crop a photo, select the Crop option, move the four corner handles—and/or drag the whole crop box first—to isolate the part of the image you want to crop out; then select OK.

5. Click or tap the right arrow as many times as necessary (depending on how many photos and/or videos you have to get through) to get back to the Camera app.

6. Right-click or press and hold on the main camera screen and select Video Mode to take a video. Click or tap anywhere and you'll see a three-second countdown appear and then the video will begin recording. Click or tap to stop recording the video.

7. To view a video, click or tap the arrow button at left. It will be there among any pictures or other videos you've taken. Keep hitting the arrow button until you get to it. Click the Play button to view the video. To trim a video, right-click or press and hold on the screen, select Trim, move the white slider on the video's timeline to where you want it, and select OK.

8. Right-click or press and hold on the screen and select Camera Options to change photo resolution, your audio device, and toggle video stabilization on or off. Click or tap the More link to change the brightness, contrast, and flicker settings.

Read Documents with Reader

Windows 8 includes the Reader app for viewing PDF and XPS files. XPS files are not as well-known as PDF files, but really they're just a Microsoft equivalent to the PDF format. Reader isn't on the Start screen but is listed in All Apps. Here's how to open and read a document with Reader:

1. Start Reader from All Apps by right-clicking or pressing and holding on an empty section of the Start screen and selecting All Apps.

2. Click or tap the Browse tile. If a document opens and there is no Browse tile, right-click or press and hold on the screen and choose Open to find the Browse tile.

 After you have read at least one document, it will appear next to the Browse tile under the Recent heading and you'll then be able to click or tap it there to read it without browsing to it.

3. Click or tap on folders until you find the file you want. When you do, select the file and then click or tap Open. The document appears in Reader in linear, with pages in addition to the first appearing below it.

4. Use the scrollbar at right to scroll down through the document and read it. With a mouse, you can also use your scroll wheel.

5. Click or tap the plus or minus icons in the lower right of the screen to zoom in or out.

 You can zoom so far out that you can see all of the pages onscreen together, making it much easier to jump around in a document.

6. Right-click or press and hold on the screen to summon these options, from left to right:

- **Find**   Search for text within the document.

- **Two Pages**   Switch your view to two pages onscreen side by side. Instead of scrolling down, you'll tap arrows at the right and left of the screen to view the next or previous two pages, respectively.

- **One Page**   Similar to Two Pages but with a single page onscreen only.

- **Continuous**   All pages appears in one column; additional pages are below the first and are accessible by scrolling down.

- **Open**   Open another document.

- **Save As**   Save the file.

- **More**   Here you can choose to rotate the file, view information about it, bookmark a page, or close a file.

 Access the Settings charm and choose Options if you want to change the reading direction to left to right if you're reading Arabic or Farsi, for example.

7

Surf the Net

With Windows 8, Microsoft has continued Windows' long history of integrating the Web into the PC operating system. I've discussed some of the cooler new Web features such as Sync, SkyDrive, and the People app in other chapters. In this chapter, I show you how to set up your Internet connection, how to browse the Web with both the desktop and Windows 8–style versions of Internet Explorer, and where to get Mozilla Firefox or Google Chrome.

Set Up Your Internet Connection

Setting up your Internet connection in Windows 8 will be different depending on your particular setup and hardware. Typically, the process involves configuring a broadband router from your Internet service provider, and the specifics of that task differ dramatically depending on not just the provider but also the type of hardware involved. However, after you get your connection up, the process of connecting Windows 8 to an active Internet connection will be the same. Here's how:

1. Ensure that your wired connection is plugged in (the Ethernet cable) or that your computer's wireless is turned on.

2. Access the Settings charm. The Settings pane slides in from the right.

Now You Know — Microsoft Has Been Trying to Integrate the Internet for Years

The concept behind active, constantly updating apps is not new to Windows, although Windows 8 marks the first time Microsoft has done so in a fashion other than simply adding self-updating Internet-enabled apps on the desktop itself. Microsoft Windows 98 introduced Active Desktop as Web applets for the desktop. Windows Vista attempted this same thing with gadgets, which were basically minor programs that also included dynamically updating Internet content on the desktop. In Windows 8, tiles provide constantly refreshing Internet content on the new Start screen overlay instead of on the desktop itself, although some of them, such as the People tile, do also infiltrate the desktop when updates come around.

3. Click or tap Network. The icon may not say Network on it, but it's the top left icon of the six sitting at the bottom of the Settings pane.

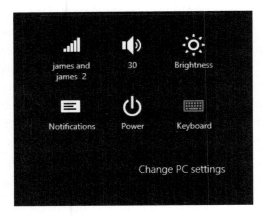

4. Select the network that is yours; you need to know its name.

5. Click or tap Connect and enter a password if prompted. If you're accessing a private network, it should have a password, but if you're accessing a public network such as at Starbucks, you won't need one.

6. Check the Connect Automatically check box if you want Windows to automatically connect to this network in the future.

7. Click or tap Connect again to connect to your network.

After your connection is set up, it's time to surf the Web. Your first default browser is Internet Explorer 10, and you need to use it at the very least to go get your favorite browser as described at the end of the chapter.

Surf the Web with Internet Explorer 10

Surfing the Web in Windows 8 can be a very different experience than with previous versions of Windows, depending on whether you use a Windows 8–style browser or a desktop browser. Because Internet Explorer is the default browser for Windows 8, the following sections show you how to surf in Internet Explorer 10 Windows 8–style and desktop versions, respectively.

Surf the Web with the Internet Explorer Windows 8–Style app

Internet Explorer has been totally redesigned as a Windows 8–style application for the Windows 8 version of Internet Explorer 10. The experience little resembles a regular desktop browser except for the appearance of the address bar and the Web page itself. Here's how to use Internet Explorer 10's Windows 8–style version:

1. Access the Internet Explorer Windows 8–style app by clicking or tapping the Internet Explorer tile on your Start screen. You may have to scroll or swipe right to find it, but it is near the left side by default.

If the Internet Explorer tile has for some reason been deleted, right-click or press and hold an empty portion of the Start screen and choose All Apps to access it under the main list at the left.

2. Your default home page appears. You'll see the address bar while the page loads. When it finishes loading the address bar disappears.

3. Right-click or press and hold on the screen to summon the address bar at the bottom of the screen and the list of tabs at the top of the screen, as shown in Figure 7-1.

 After a few seconds of inactivity with your fingers or mouse, the address bar and tabs pane at the top of the screen disappear. To make the address bar reappear, right-click or swipe up from the bottom of the screen.

4. Click or tap the address bar and type in a Web address and then click or tap the Forward (right-facing) arrow at the right side of the bar at the bottom of the screen. Your Web page loads.

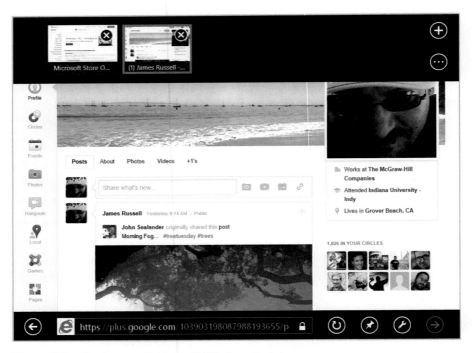

Figure 7-1   *The Internet Explorer 10 Windows 8–style app*

Although at first it may seem a bit strange to have your Forward and Back buttons split up on opposite sides of the screen, bear in mind that Internet Explorer Windows 8–style's interface is optimized for touchscreens and Microsoft assumes if you're using a tablet you'll have one thumb in the lower left and one in the lower right. It's the way you type on a tablet using the split keyboard and it's how you go back and forward in Internet Explorer 10 Windows 8–style, too.

5. Click or tap a link to move to a new page.

6. To go back a page, click or tap the Back button, which is the left-pointing arrow in the lower left corner of the screen. On a touchscreen, simply swipe from the left edge of the screen towards the center to go back.

7. To reload a page, click or tap the Refresh button, which has a circular arrow on it and is located to the immediate right of the address bar.

 Internet Explorer's Windows 8–style incarnation does not support add-ons at all. If you want to use add-ons, you'll have to use Internet Explorer for desktop.

After you've mastered the basics of using the browser, here are a few tips to really kickstart your Internet Explorer 10 Windows 8–style experience:

- **Flip Forward** If you load a page and Internet Explorer sees an obvious page to move from the current page to, the Forward arrow at the right side of the screen will light up. Tap the arrow to move forward to whatever page Internet Explorer predicts you'll want to go to. This feature can be enabled or disabled via the Settings pane (see the "Configure Internet Explorer Windows 8–Style" section later in the chapter). Flip Forward only works in the Internet Explorer Windows 8–style app.

- **Pin to Start** This button is to the right of the Reload button and has a thumbtack on it. Select it to pin a Web page to the Start screen. Before pinning, Internet Explorer gives you the option to rename the tile. Some pages are interactive so that the tile on the Start screen will update you when there are new tweets as long as you have given Internet Explorer permission to notify you (see the "Configure Internet Explorer Windows 8–Style" section later in the chapter).

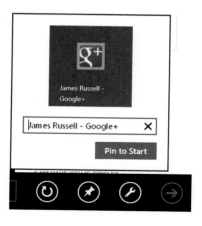

- **Page Tools Button** To the right of the Pin to Start button is a button with an icon of a wrench on it called the Page Tools button. Click this to access these options:

    - **Get App for this Site** Some pages have apps in the Windows Store associated with them. If that's the case with the site you're on, this option will be enabled. Otherwise, it will be grayed out.

    - **Find on Page** Search for text on the current page.

    - **View on the desktop** If you want to view the current page in the desktop version of Internet Explorer, choose this item to instantly go to the desktop Internet Explorer, as discussed in the next section.

Surf the Web with the Internet Explorer Desktop

Internet Explorer 10 for the desktop is very similar in appearance to Internet Explorer 9 in terms of setup: the Back and Forward buttons are together in the upper left corner of the screen, the address bar is across the top of the screen, and the Home, Favorites, and Tools buttons are in the upper right, as shown in Figure 7-2.

If you've used a desktop browser in the past on any computer, you may be familiar with Internet Explorer 9 and other basics for browsing, but here's a primer on version 10 of the browser:

1. Start Internet Explorer from the desktop by clicking or tapping its icon. Alternatively, if you're in Internet Explorer, Windows 8–style you can choose View on the Desktop by clicking or tapping the Page Tools button in the lower right of the Internet Explorer interface.

2. Click or tap the address bar at the top of the screen and type a URL such as "google.com" (without quotes) into it. Press ENTER to go to a page.

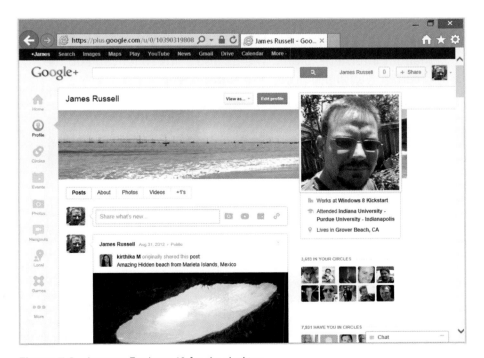

Figure 7-2 *Internet Explorer 10 for the desktop*

3. Click the Back button in the very upper left of the window (left-facing arrow) to go back to a previous page. Click Forward (right-facing arrow) just to the right of it to go forward to a page you previously clicked Back on.

4. Click the Home button (the little house icon in the upper right region of the window) to go to your default page that starts when you start your browser.

5. Click the Refresh button in the very right corner of the address bar (it's a circular arrow) to reload the current page.

6. Click the Favorites button (it's a star in the very upper right of the window) to access your favorite pages, feeds, and any Web browsing history you have.

7. Click the Settings icon (it's the cog wheel in the upper right of the window) to access a menu. From here you can access menus for printing options, file-related options, page zoom, and safety features. You also can manage add-ons, developer tools, access Internet Options (discussed in the "Configure Internet Explorer Desktop" section later in the chapter), and get information about Internet Explorer. There's also a link to let you add the currently displayed site to the Start screen.

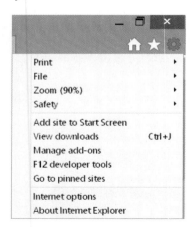

Configure Internet Explorer

You can configure both versions of Internet Explorer, but by far most of the configuration for both has to be done via the desktop version. All settings, such as security settings, not having to do specifically with how the page is viewed need to be configured in desktop mode. Those settings apply to Internet Explorer in both browser modes. The following sections show you how to configure both versions of Internet Explorer.

Configure the Internet Explorer Windows 8–Style app

The Internet Explorer 10 Windows 8–style app has a very limited amount of settings available to configure. Here's how to configure the few things you can in Internet Explorer:

1. Access the Settings charm while viewing the Internet Explorer Windows 8–style app. The Settings pane slides in from the right.

2. Click or tap the Internet Options link near the top of the pane.

 The other three links are About, Help, and Permissions, and lead only to information about Internet Explorer, help documentation, and the ability to enable or disable Internet Explorer's ability to notify you throughout the Windows interface, such as notifying you of new tweets if you add a Twitter page to your Start screen.

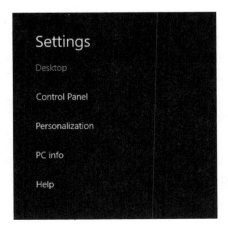

3. Choose from the available options to give or revoke Internet Explorer's permission to allow sites to access your location, change the zoom level, or clear browsing history.

Configure Internet Explorer Desktop

Internet Explorer 10 on the desktop offers many more options to configure than Internet Explorer Windows 8–style, including your general, privacy, security, and advanced settings. Here's how to configure Internet Explorer for desktop:

1. Start Internet Explorer 10 for desktop.

2. Right-click or press and hold on the toolbar to the right of the address bar to access a list of toolbars you can enable or disable in Internet Explorer. Check or uncheck each to enable or disable it. Toolbars available include

   - **Menu bar**   The old menus (File, Edit, and so on) can be restored by adding this bar. You can also toggle this toolbar on and off via the ALT key.

   - **Favorites bar**   Choose from your favorites without having to click the Favorites button.

   - **Command bar**   Access advanced commands and get quicker access to items on the Tools menu.

   - **Status bar**   View the status information of loading pages or see URLs by hovering over links at the bottom of the window.

   - **Bing search bar**   Search Bing from your browser window.

3. Click or tap the Tools icon (it looks like a cog wheel in the upper right) and choose Internet Options. The Internet Options window appears, as shown in Figure 7-3.

4. Choose from the following tabs to configure different types of items on each:

   - **General**   Change your home page, customize what tabs start when you start your browser, set your browser to delete browsing history on exit, or change link colors.

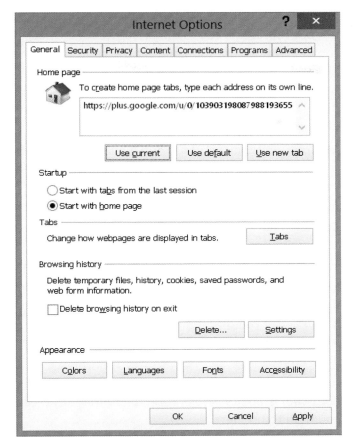

Figure 7-3 *The Internet Options window*

- **Security**   This tab allows you to use a slider to raise or lower the browser's security level. High trusts nothing about any Web site at all and Medium trusts most Web sites but disables unsigned ActiveX controls. Medium High is less stringent than High but more so than Medium and is the default setting.

You can also click the Custom Level button to configure your own level, but do so only if you're very advanced in knowledge about programming security.

- **Privacy**   This tab has a slider similar to the one on the Security tab but represents cookie privacy instead. Low accepts all cookies without question and High accepts none whatsoever. The default setting is Medium High. You can also configure whether Internet Explorer shares your location, enable or disable the pop-up window blocker, and choose whether to disable toolbars and extensions when in Private mode.

- **Content**   On this tab you'll find a link to Family Safety, SSL certificates for encrypted browsing, text field auto-complete based on Internet Explorer's guess about what you're typing, and settings for feed and Web slices.

- **Connections**   This tab allows you to configure more Internet connections or change LAN settings.

- **Programs**   Here you can customize what programs Internet Explorer works with to perform actions that the browser doesn't perform itself, such as e-mail programs and HTML editors. You can also manage add-ons and configure Internet Explorer to always start in a certain mode, such as in desktop mode.

- **Advanced**   Fine-tune which types of security settings, hardware graphics acceleration, and other advanced options you wish to use here.

5. Click or tap Apply to apply changes and then click or tap OK to close the window.

Change Your Default Browser

After you're up and running with Internet Explorer, you may choose to install another browser in addition to it, or you may want to use a different browser than Internet Explorer. All major browsers—most notably Internet Explorer, Firefox, and Chrome—are, as of this writing, in the works for Windows 8–style interfaces.

The desktop interfaces are the same you've been used to if you've used either browser before, and are similar to Internet Explorer 10 desktop. To switch to Mozilla Firefox, you'll need to download and install the browser from www.getfirefox.com. To use Google Chrome as your browser, you'll need to download and install it from www.google .com/chrome.

To change your default browser, follow these steps:

1. Access the Settings charm and choose Control Panel.

2. Select Programs and then Default Programs.

3. Click or tap Set Your Default Programs. The Set Default Programs window appears.

4. Click either Firefox or Chrome in the left pane and click Set This Program as Default.

5. Click OK.

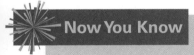

Now You Know   **Your Default Browser Runs Windows 8–Style Apps**

If you want to use Firefox or Chrome in Windows 8–style mode, you will have to change your default browser to one of those browsers from Internet Explorer, and until you change it back you won't be able to use Internet Explorer or any other browser in Windows 8–style mode either.

8

Share with Social Media and Instant Messaging

Windows 8 integrates social media and instant messaging—in particular in relation to social media—into the new Windows 8–style interface in several major ways: the Messaging and People apps, the Share charm, and the File Explorer Share tab, which is discussed in Chapter 4.

Windows 8 includes two new apps that, together with the Mail app, are together the hub for Windows 8 social communication. From instant messaging via Windows Live Messenger or Facebook Messenger, or communicating via e-mail, phone, or social media apps such as Facebook and Twitter, you can do it all from these using three apps. The Mail app, discussed in Chapter 6, is simply the e-mail piece—the Messaging and People apps essentially make up the rest of the communications platform between them.

In this chapter I'll show you how to set up the Messaging and People apps and how to use them and the Windows 8 Share charm to share your content with whoever you want. Because the Share charm really is the key to Windows 8 sharing—even if it is in its infancy and has yet to reach its potential—I'll show you some of the various ways you can use the charm to share content with your world. Finally, because Windows 8 is so new, many services like Yahoo! Instant Messenger and Google Talk don't hook into it yet, so I'll also tell you where to get those.

Configure and Explore the People App

Think of the People app as a social media hub where you can view LinkedIn, Facebook, Twitter, and more networks under the same interface, as well as see the contact information for all those contacts in one place. It's actually a pretty killer app. The following sections show you how to set up the People app to integrate your contacts.

 If you ever find yourself lost in the People app—that is, seemingly unable to go back to the home page—right-click or press and hold on an empty spot on the screen and select the Home button.

Add Accounts to the People App

The People app is where Microsoft consolidates all of the contacts you have for every account you add to it. At the time of the Windows 8 launch, the People app supports Microsoft (obviously), Google, Facebook, Twitter, LinkedIn, Hotmail (including @MSN.com, @Live.com, and @Hotmail.com), Exchange, Office 365, and Outlook.com accounts.

Here's how to add an account to the People app:

1. Open the People app by clicking or tapping its tile on the Start screen.

2. Access the Settings charm, select Accounts, and then select Add an account from the resulting pane.

3. Select the type of account—for example, choose Facebook.

4. Type in the username and password for the account you want to add and click OK. The contacts associated with that account will be retrieved and populate your People app, as shown in Figure 8-1. The interface is similar to a notebook-style address book. See the "Contact People" section later in this chapter for more on the People app.

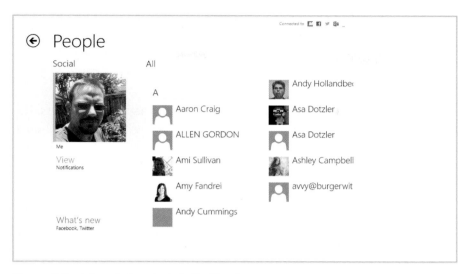

Figure 8-1 *Integrated contacts in the People app*

View Social Media Contacts and Notifications

The People app allows you to view basic information about your social media contacts and link instantly to their profiles via your default Web browser. To view information about a contact in the People app, follow these steps:

1. Open the People app by clicking or tapping its tile on the Start screen.

2. Scroll through the list of contacts and select a person's listing. You can also just start typing and the Search pane will appear. Make sure People is selected in the list and you can search for a contact by name. The person's listing doubles as a link to information about them. Click or tap the name and a page appears for that person. You'll see three sections from left to right:

   - **Contact**   Depending on whether the person is online via Facebook or Windows Messenger and how much contact information they've made available to you via the various networks you have them in, you will see different contact information. For example, if they have their phone number set to be viewable to friends on Facebook, you will see a Call link here with their phone number next to it which you could use to start a Skype call with that person, for example. Similarly, you'll see the ability to send a message if they are online on Facebook Messenger or a Send E-mail link if you have their e-mail address. You can also map their address, if they have provided it, or click View Profile to bring up their full profile in your default browser, as shown in Figure 8-2.

- **What's New** View this section to see the person's latest updates from whatever networks you have them in. Click the View All link near the top of the section to see all of their recent posts.

- **Photos** Click the link near the top of the page that says the number of albums the person has, to view the person's Facebook photo albums.

From the People app home page, click View Notifications below your picture to view your new notifications. You can reply to them just as you could on Facebook.

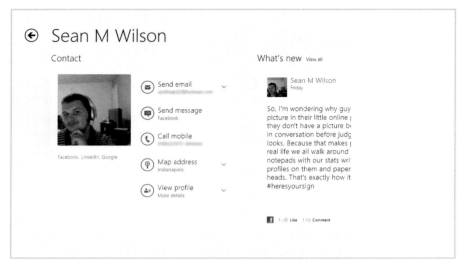

Figure 8-2 *View a contact.*

Configure and Explore the Messaging App

Related to the People app but still distinct is the Messaging app. Messaging doesn't support all of the same services that the People app does. Indeed, Messaging only supports Windows Messenger and Facebook Messenger. Your Windows Messenger account is configured as soon as you log in to the Messaging app with the Microsoft account you're signed in to Windows 8 with. At the most, you may have to input your username and password when first opening the app. To add a Facebook account to the Messaging app, follow these steps:

1. Open the Messaging app by clicking or tapping on its tile on the Start screen.

2. Access the Settings charm, select Accounts near the top of the Settings pane, and then select Add an Account.

3. Select Facebook and choose Connect when the next window appears asking for permission to access your account. If you're not logged in to Facebook in your default browser, you will have to log in to Facebook before you'll see the Connect button. Microsoft connects Facebook and brings up the Messaging app main screen shown in Figure 8-3.

Figure 8-3   *The Messaging app*

Microsoft announced as this book was being completed that Skype will soon be integrated with—and eventually completely replace—Windows Messenger.

Contact People

After you set up the People and Messaging apps, it's time to start contacting people with them. Here's how to contact someone via the Messaging app:

Recent messages are listed at the left side of the window. Simply click one to pick the conversation back up.

1. Select the Send a New Message text box at the top left of the app and search for the contact's name. When their name appears below the text box, click or tap it. The person appears in the Messaging app with their information at left and any recent messages between you and them are visible on the right.

2. Type a message into your message field at the bottom of the window. Press ENTER to send the message. Messages appear at the top of the window at first and then move down, with older messages moving off of the screen at the top. Messages from you appear against a gray background and messages from the person you're chatting with appear against a purple background color that matches the color of the Messaging app's tile. You can right-click or press and hold on an empty part of the screen and choose Invite to e-mail someone and ask them to join your contacts.

Click the smiley face to the right of your text input field to choose from Microsoft's list of emoticons.

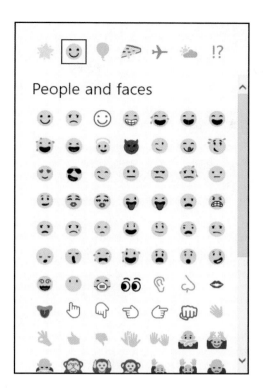

Receive Messages

Obviously you don't have to do anything to receive a message except be logged in to the Messaging app, but you should know that when you do receive a message, Windows notifies you wherever you are in the operating system via a tiny notification pane in the upper right corner of the screen with an accompanying "ding" sound—Microsoft calls this type of notification a *toast*. Click or tap on this pane before it disappears to be taken to the Messaging app to interact with the person who messaged you.

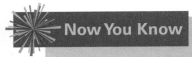

Facebook Messenger Can Become the Bane of Your Existence

Together with the Mail and Calendar apps discussed in Chapter 6, Windows 8 reduces the need for several legacy Windows apps significantly. For example, Windows Messenger and Facebook Messenger are both covered by the Messaging app, so you don't need the standalone apps anymore.

That said, with the right configuration of software, you could be notified five or more times on your computer every time you get a Facebook message. Think about it: Facebook Messenger has its own app now—AIM, YIM, and the standalone Windows Messenger allow you to connect to and chat with Facebook friends, plus the Messaging app is likely already configured for Facebook. Follow these guidelines so the Facebook Messenger notification cacophony doesn't become your life:

- Figure out your preferred method of getting Facebook messages. For this example, we'll say it's the Messaging app described earlier in this chapter. If you choose another method, exclude it from the following items and instead delete your account from it.

- Do not set YIM, AIM, or any other service such as Trillian or Adium to connect to Facebook chat, or they too will ping you each time you get a message.

- You don't need the separate Windows Messenger client because it's already integrated into the Messaging app, but if for some reason you do have it, don't set it to connect to Facebook. That's just one more app that will notify you when you get a Facebook message.

- Do not install Facebook Messenger for Windows if you have the Messaging app set up. It's redundant, and if you do so (surprise), both programs will ping you with new Facebook messages.

- Don't set up Facebook notifications in your browser—for example, extensions for Chrome—or they too will ping you when you get a message.

- Lastly, do not have the Facebook page open unnecessarily, because it too will ping you when you get a message.

Change Messaging Availability

You can change your availability status for both Facebook Messenger and Windows Messenger from Invisible so no one can see that you are online or chat with you, to Available, where people can see you and chat with you. Changing availability in the Messaging app is simple:

1. Right-click or press and hold on an empty section of the Messaging app screen. You can also swipe down from the top of the screen or up from the bottom with your finger.

2. Select Status and choose Available or Invisible.

Share with the Share Charm

The Share charm was discussed in Chapter 1. At the time this book was written, just prior to the Windows 8 launch, sharing via the Share charm work in the People app but not in Messaging. Here's how to share a contact via the People app and the Share charm:

1. Launch People by clicking or tapping the tile on your Start screen.

2. Browse to a contact, select it, and then access the Share charm. At the time of this writing, Mail was the only option by default. Click or tap it.

3. Type in a message in the field just under the title bar at the top of the pane and select the circular Send button to send the person's contact information via e-mail.

Following are a few more examples of how you can use the Share charm to share in Windows 8. Note that all of these apps are Windows Store apps:

- From the Calendar app, open an event and select the content in that event, such as time, date, or description. Access the Share charm and select Mail from the Share pane to mail the event information to someone.

Now You Know **The Share Charm Doesn't Always Work**

When you access the Share charm, the pane will often appear just to say you can't share anything—and this is the case with *all* desktop apps. Chances are that Microsoft will dramatically increase its usefulness as more non-Microsoft software vendors such as Google and Apple develop Windows Store apps for services such as Google Play and iTunes and "hook into" the Share charm to allow you to easily share things to social media sites. In the meantime, become accustomed to using it when it is helpful so that as new apps come out using it, you know to look for it.

- From the Music app, open a song, artist, or album and access the Share charm to share that song to Facebook or with a person from the People or Mail apps.

- From the Photos app, select a photo and access the Share charm to share that photo to SkyDrive or the Mail app.

- From the Video app, select a movie or television show and access the Share charm to share it with Facebook, Mail, or People recipients.

- From the Mail app, open an e-mail and select the content in an e-mail that you want to share via e-mail. Access the Share charm and select Mail from the Share pane to mail that information to someone.

- From the Camera app, snap a photo or a video, select it, and access the Share charm to share the photo or video to SkyDrive or a Mail recipient.

- From the Weather app, access the Share charm and select Mail from the Share pane to post weather information to Facebook or share it with a person from the People or Mail apps.

Messaging with Desktop Apps

Because Windows 8 is so new, companies are still working on Windows Store apps, and for this reason apps like Messaging in particular show a lot of potential to replace desktop apps but simply haven't yet. As mentioned earlier, as of the Windows 8 launch, Messaging supports only Windows Messenger and Facebook Messenger. That's a lot of services that it doesn't include, such as Yahoo! Instant Messenger, Google Talk, AOL Instant Messenger, and Skype, which Microsoft now owns and the company has said will replace Windows Messenger. In this section I'll show you where to go to get those messaging apps that, at least at the time of this writing, the Windows 8 Messaging app doesn't support:

- **Yahoo! Instant Messenger** One of the most popular instant messaging platforms to this day, the YIM client offers many features similar to Skype and Google Talk, including Web phone calls, free video conferencing, and a full-featured messaging client. Get YIM at http://messenger.yahoo.com/.

- **Google Talk** Integrating what was known as Google Chat in the past, Google Talk is available to Gmail users and is a mobile and desktop instant messaging, Web calling, texting, and an advanced video conferencing service platform that includes *hangouts* of up to 10 people video conferencing together. Google Talk is available from www.google.com/talk/.

- **AOL Instant Messenger** AIM was one of the first major instant messaging clients, and it, like YIM, can integrate Facebook chat, too. AIM still has a strong following and can be downloaded from www.aim.com/.

- **Skype** Microsoft recently bought Skype and has said that it will be fully integrated in Office 2013. Skype is freely available in the Windows Store or the desktop version is available at www.skype.com/.

9

View and Manage Photos

Photographs and images are important parts of many people's personal and work lives, and Microsoft has made Windows 8 the most photo-friendly version of Windows yet. In this chapter I'll get you up to speed on how to view, manage, and modify your photos and images.

 With the integration of the Office ribbon-style UI into the File Explorer interface, you now have many more options than you used to when working with your photos and images. The Pictures library is really a combination view of one or more folders that contain pictures or other images and you can customize it at will. In Chapter 4, I describe how to access, manage, and configure Pictures and other libraries.

View Photos and Images

You have several ways to view your images and photos in Windows 8:

- **View Photos in the Photos Windows Store app** The newest way to work with photos, the Windows Store Photos app lets you view and perform only a very few tasks with photos. At the time of Windows 8's release, very little in the way of photo editing exists in the Photos app.

- **View Photos with Windows Photo Viewer**   Windows Photo Viewer is not terribly robust in terms of features, but it does allow basic photo-management capabilities such as rotating photos.
- **View Photos in a Slideshow**   View photos in any folder in full-screen slideshow format.
- **Send Photos to Another Device**   Play slideshows on TVs or other compatible devices.

In the following sections I show you how to do these things as well as how to get information about your photos via File Explorer.

View Photos in the Photos App

Viewing photos in the Photos Windows Store app is the newest way to access your photos, and the app shows you photos from various potential sources. The overall experience feels like a slideshow view with you tapping or clicking arrows at either side of the screen to flip between photos. Open the Photos app by tapping or clicking its tile on the Start screen. The Photos app appears, as shown in Figure 9-1.

Figure 9-1   *The Photos app*

You'll see the following five sources for photos along the bottom of the screen, each represented by a picture within that source. Click or tap any of these items to see and work with the photos within:

- **Pictures Library**   All photos in your Pictures library will be displayed here. Choose and right-click or press and hold on an image to see buttons that allow you to delete the file, start a slideshow, or set it as your Desktop background, lock screen, or as the Photo app background image.

- **Facebook**   If you've logged into Facebook, you can view your Facebook photos here. When you click the Facebook item, you'll see your various albums. Click an album and then click a photo to be able to work with the photo; you can right-click or press and hold on a photo to start a slideshow or set it as your Desktop background, lock screen, or as the Photo app background image. You will also see a button to view the image in Facebook.

- **SkyDrive**   If you have photos on your SkyDrive, you'll see them here. Choose and right-click or press and hold on an image to see buttons that allow you to start a slideshow or set it as your Desktop background, lock screen, or as the Photo app background image. You also see a button to view the image on SkyDrive.

- **Flickr**   Log in to Flickr to see photos from that service here. Choose and right-click or press and hold on an image to see buttons that allow you to start a slideshow or set it as your Desktop background, lock screen, or as the Photo app background image. You also see a button to view the image on SkyDrive.

 You may have to add the Microsoft e-mail address you use for your Windows 8 Microsoft account to your Flickr account and confirm the e-mail address by replying to an e-mail from Flickr before you can connect to Flickr successfully.

- **Device Photos**   If you have a device such as a smartphone connected to your PC that has photos on it, you'll see those here.

Right-click or press and hold on the main Photos screen to see an Import button. Use this to import photos from an external device.

View Photos with Windows Photo Viewer

If you want to view a photo in Windows Photo Viewer, you cannot simply double-click or double-tap the file. Doing so will open the file in the Windows Store Photos app by default. You have two major options for viewing a file in Windows Photo Viewer depending on how you like to use your computer:

- **Via the File Explorer Ribbon** Open File Explorer, open the ribbon with the downward-pointing arrow near the upper right corner of the window if necessary, and select the Home tab. Click the file's item or thumbnail and then click the downward-facing arrow next to the little blue image icon in the Open section of the ribbon and choose Windows Photo Viewer from the resulting list.

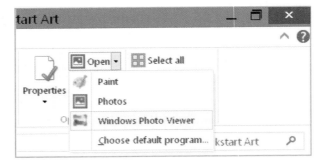

- **Via Context Menu** Right-click or press and hold the photo file or thumbnail, choose Open With, and then select Windows Photo Viewer.

After opening a file, you'll see it in the viewer, as shown in Figure 9-2.

Figure 9-2 *A photo open in Windows Photo Viewer*

The following tools on the interface allow you to work with the file. Across the top of the window you see the following five items (obviously Windows Photo Viewer hasn't been ribbonized if it still has menus):

- **File** Delete, copy, view properties for, or exit viewing a photo.
- **Print** Print a photo or order photo prints via Microsoft's partners, which include CVS, Kodak, and Shutterfly among others.
- **E-mail** E-mail the photo to someone.
- **Burn** Burn the photo to disc.
- **Open** Open the current photo in Paint or another program.

Across the bottom of the window you'll see buttons with which you can change the view of the photo. From left to right the buttons are

- **Change the Display Size** Use the slider to zoom in or out on the image.
- **Actual Size** Select this to return the image to its default size.

- **Previous**   View the previous photo in the folder.
- **Play Slide Show**   Start a slideshow using this image and other images in the folder.
- **Next**   View the next photo in the folder.
- **Rotate Counterclockwise**   Rotate the image 90 degrees counterclockwise (left).
- **Rotate Clockwise**   Rotate the image 90 degrees clockwise (right).
- **Delete**   Delete the photo.

View a Slideshow

You can view photos in any folder as a full-screen slideshow. The following are several ways of viewing a slideshow:

- **Via the Windows Store Photos app**   While in the Photos app, select a folder, right-click or press and hold on a blank spot of the screen, and then click or tap the Slideshow button that appears. This method is quick but provides absolutely no method of customizing the slideshow. Press any key, move your mouse, tap the screen, or swipe in any direction to stop the slideshow.

- **Via the Pictures library in File Explorer (or any library optimized for pictures)**   Navigate to and select the folder you want to start a slideshow from. Click the Picture Tools tab on the ribbon and then click the Slideshow button. Right-click or press and hold the screen to summon a menu allowing you to customize the slideshow. Using this menu, you can play, pause, exit, change the speed of, loop indefinitely, and shuffle the order of the images in the slideshow.

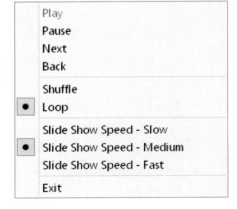

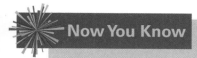

**Change Your Default Viewer
to Another Program**

If you don't want photos opening in the less-capable Photos app, which you can't do a lot with other than view, you can choose to have them open in Windows Photo Viewer (or another program) easily:

1. Right-click or press and hold the photo file or thumbnail and then choose Open With.

2. Select Choose Default Program and a little unnamed window appears listing apps on your computer that are capable of opening photos. At the bottom of the list, click More Options to see even more apps that technically can open photos but that Microsoft thinks you are less likely to open photos with, such as WordPad.

3. Choose Windows Photo Viewer or whichever program you want to open photos with.

Press CTRL on a keyboard to exit the slideshow.

- **Via Windows Photo Viewer** If you have a photo open in Windows Photo Viewer and want to start a slideshow with it and whatever other photos are in the same folder, simply click the button in the center of the circle at the bottom middle of the screen. The slideshow will start. Right-click or press and hold the screen to summon a menu allowing you to customize the slideshow using the same menu described in the previous bullet.

Send Photos to Another Device

Microsoft's Play To feature debuted in Windows 7 and lets you play videos, music, or photo slideshows on TVs, stereos, or other PCs or devices that are compatible with Windows 8's Play To feature. You can send photos to another device via the Pictures library in File Explorer (or any library optimized for pictures) as follows:

1. Navigate to photos you want to play to on another device in File Explorer.

2. Click the Picture Tools tab on the File Explorer ribbon.

3. Click the Play To icon, choose a device to play the files to, and select that device.

Get Information About Photos in File Explorer

You have three major options to get information about your images in File Explorer. The following options are listed in the order of how much information they give you, from least to most:

- **Hover over the image** Hover your mouse cursor over an image. In the tooltip that appears will be listed the file type, the date the photo was taken, the file's rating, its dimensions, and its size. There is no equivalent for touchscreens.

- **Use the Details View** Choose the Details view on the View tab to see several columns next to each file, including by default its name, the date it was taken, any tags associated with it, and its file rating. By default, hovering your mouse cursor over an image shows you more information than this, but if you click the Add Columns button in the Current View section of the View tab on the File Explorer ribbon you can add more columns by selecting them from the list that appears.

- **Check the image's properties** Right-click or press and hold on any image, choose Properties, and then select the Details tab to see as much information as Windows can possibly show you about that file. Figure 9-3 shows the Details tab for the image I captured for the screenshot for Figure 9-2.

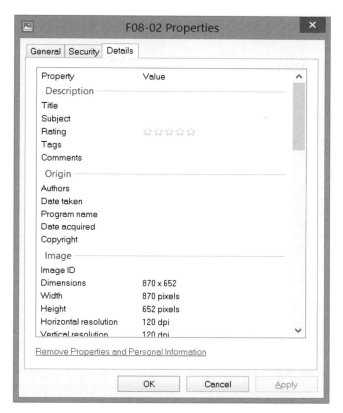

Figure 9-3   *Viewing an image's properties*

Manage Your Photos

Chapter 4 describes how to work with photos as files within the Pictures library. In the following sections I show you how to set an image as your desktop background as well as how to edit, resize, and crop photos.

I discuss printing photos in Chapter 5.

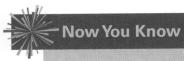

Change Photo File Names Once

Cameras are lousy at naming pictures, typically naming them by number as in "0101, 0102, 0103" and so forth. Renaming photos can be a huge chore, so it's wise to make changes to file names as soon as you upload a given batch of pictures so you don't have to do so all at once later. Make sure to back up the renamed versions so you never have to go through the process again. You can also use programs like NameWiz (available at http://download.cnet.com/NameWiz/3000-2248_4-10004931.html) to help rename numerous files simultaneously, but if you like to name your photos based on the content of the photo ("Jenny Eating Her Bunny," for example), NameWiz won't be able to help you much.

Set an Image as Your Desktop Background

Set an image as your desktop background by right-clicking or pressing and holding on a picture thumbnail or item and choosing or tapping Set as Desktop Background. You can also click a photo in the Pictures library in File Explorer, click the photo, select the Picture Tools tab, and click the Set as Background button. You can only do this in Windows 8–style mode.

Edit Photos with Paint

Paint has been a part of Windows almost since Windows began, and it is still the default photo and image-editing software for Windows. Like File Explorer did in Windows 8, Paint got ribbonized in Windows 7 and that interface remains in Windows 8. Figure 9-4 shows Paint with a picture of your author open.

The following sections show you the very basics of photo editing with Paint—specifically how to resize and crop your images.

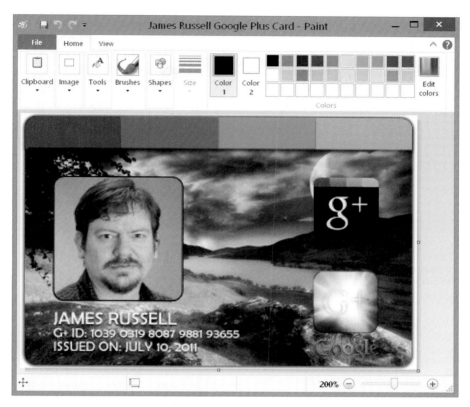

Figure 9-4   *Microsoft's Paint program*

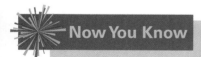 **Save an Image of Your Screen**

Called "screenshots," because back in the 1980s people actually had to snap photos of computer screens to be able to use an image of a screen in a technical book Since the 1990s, Windows has included a very simple method of capturing an image of your current screen and saving it in Paint or another capable application. In fact, I used this process to capture images for this book. The process requires a

(continued)

keyboard with a PRINT SCREEN key (sometimes labeled as PRTSC/SYSREQ). Here's how:

1. Navigate to the screen you want to capture and set it up as you want it to look.

2. Press the PRTSC key to capture the entire screen or press ALT-PRTSC to capture only the active window.

3. Open Paint and press CTRL-V to paste the image from the Windows clipboard into Paint.

4. Work with the file as necessary and then save it using the Save As option on the File tab.

Resize Photos

Resizing photos in Paint is pretty simple:

1. Open a file in Paint and click the Select tool on the ribbon.

2. Right-click or press and hold on the photo and choose Resize. The Resize and Skew window appears.

3. Click the Percentage or Pixels radio button to adjust the image size by percentage or pixels, respectively. Make sure the Maintain Aspect Ratio check box is checked if you don't want the image distorted from its default settings.

4. Change the numbers in the Horizontal and Vertical text fields as desired and click OK.

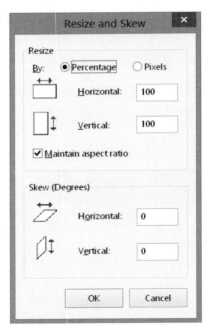

Because Paint doesn't allow you to preview before clicking OK, you may have to undo your changes (by pressing CTRL-Z or clicking the Undo button in the Quick Launch Toolbar in the extreme upper left corner of the Paint window—it's a blue arrow pointing up and left) and follow the steps again using different numbers until you get the size you want.

Crop Photos

To crop (or cut a part out of) photos in Paint, follow these steps:

1. Open the file in Paint and choose the Select tool in the ribbon.

2. Click or press and hold the image and then drag the resulting square outline down and right until you get the section of the photo you want to keep, as shown in Figure 9-5.

3. Select the Crop button on the ribbon or right click or press and hold on the crop line and select Crop from the resulting menu.

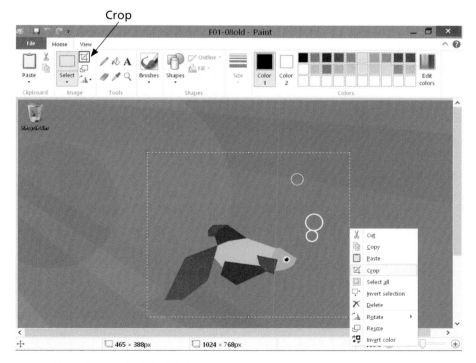

Figure 9-5 *Crop a photo in Paint*

10

Play Music and Video

Music and video are key parts of the modern computing experience, and from the Music and Video apps in Windows 8 to Windows Media Player, Microsoft gives you a lot of options for playing your media. Microsoft has also built its Xbox Music store into Windows 8, so if you have a Microsoft account you can preview and buy music right from your PC. You can also organize playlists and work with your media files from Windows Media Player. In this chapter I'll get you up to speed on the Music and Video apps as well as the very basics of configuring and using Windows Media Player.

 Chapter 4 describes managing your music and videos via File Explorer.

Explore the Music App

The Windows 8 Music app allows you to play and manage your music files in one place as well as buy new music, create and edit playlists, and more. Here's how to fire up the Music app and get comfortable with it:

1. Start the Music app by clicking or tapping its tile on the Start screen. If it's not there, right-click or press and hold on an empty part of the Start screen or swipe from the bottom or top edge toward the center of the screen, choose All Apps, and start it

Figure 10-1   *The Windows 8 Music app*

from there. The Music app appears centered on the Now Playing
section, as shown in Figure 10-1.

2. Scroll or swipe left or right to see additional sections. From
   extreme left to right, the sections are as follows:

   • **My Music**   If your music is in your My Music folder, all of
     that music will be available to you here. See the next section
     for information about playing music.

   • **Now Playing**   This section shows the song most recently
     played, or currently playing, surrounded on the bottom and
     the right by featured artists.

   • **Xbox Music Store**   Click here to buy music. See the "Buy
     Music" section later in this chapter for more information.

   • **Most Popular**   If you're interested in what's popular with
     other Xbox Music users, this section shows you what's trending
     as popular on Xbox Music.

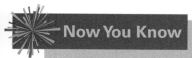

Now You Know **Give Others Access to Your Music or Videos**

If you click or tap the Videos library in the navigation pane of File Explorer and then click or tap the arrow next to it, you will see two folders: My Videos and Public Videos. The same goes for Public Music, Public Documents, and Public Pictures. Any images in the Public folders will be visible to others who have an account on your PC or others in your HomeGroup. You can also share videos with others using the Share tab while in the Videos library.

Play Music

To play a song you already have, open the song from My Music. If it isn't listed on the main Music app screen, tap the My Music link at the top of the section to view all of your music and find it by album, artist, song, or playlist. Click or tap to select a song—you'll have to click or tap twice if you tap on a multitrack album—and then click Play Song/Play Album or Add to Now Playing. If nothing is playing, in both cases the song will start playing immediately. If a song is already playing and there are songs ahead of it in the Now Playing queue, the song will play in the order it was added to the queue.

 If you don't feel like selecting anything, just click or tap the Play All Music button.

You can also play music from other sections of the Xbox Music app by clicking or tapping on an artist, song, or album. Depending on the licensing for a given song or album, you'll see different options. The most common options are Preview to play a short clip of the song, Play Album, Buy Album, Explorer Artist, and Play on Xbox 360 if you have that console as part of your home entertainment system.

To return to the main Xbox Music screen, select the Back or Home button in the upper left of the My Music page; it's only a Home button if you chose in Preferences to go straight to the My Music screen when you start the music app (see the "Configure the Music App" section later in this chapter).

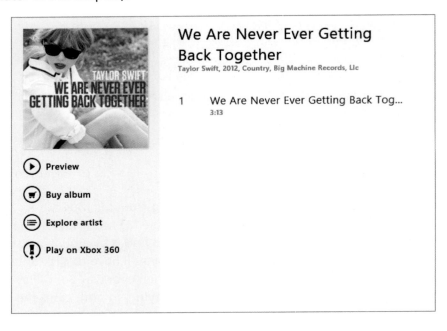

Create and Manage Playlists

Creating and using playlists lets you save groups of songs for different settings. You might have a playlist of soft music to go to sleep to, for example, or a more upbeat playlist for when guests come over for dinner. Here's how to work with playlists:

1. Select the My Music link at the top of that section.

2. Select Playlists from the menu at left.

 You can select from a drop-down list in the upper left to sort playlists by Date Changed, Date Added, or A to Z.

3. Select the New Playlist button.

4. Type in a name for the playlist and then click or tap Save.

5. Click or tap Albums, Artists, or Songs and find a song or album you want to add to the playlist.

6. Right-click or press and hold on an album, choose "Add to Playlist," and then select a playlist name to add the song or album to that playlist.

7. Add two or more songs and then click Playlists in the left menu again.

8. Select a playlist and it will appear with the songs in it.

9. Select a song and tiny up and down arrows will appear at left. Click these to move the song up or down in the playlist. To the right are the Play and Remove from Playlist buttons that you can use to accomplish those actions.

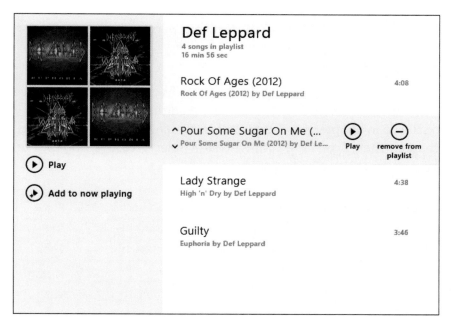

10. Right-click or swipe from the bottom or top edge toward the center of the screen to see a controls overlay. This can be used to open the current file in the app's File Explorer window, shuffle songs, repeat a song, pause or unpause play, or go to the next or previous song.

Work with Smart DJs

Microsoft has included a feature in the Music app called Smart DJs. Similar to free Internet radio apps like Pandora, Smart DJs allows you to pick an artist and have Xbox Music pick songs and artists that are related to your chosen artist and then play them in random order. The Smart DJs option is underneath the Playlists option. Just type in or select an artist and click Play to start your personalized radio station.

Buy Music

To buy a song or album, make sure you've hooked up your Xbox Live account to Windows and entered your credit card information, as discussed in Chapter 11. The process is the same as discussed in that chapter. Then, access the Settings charm, select Account, and click or tap the Enter New Credit Card button.

 Microsoft is building its Xbox Music app from its older Zune service. Mostly you'll see the title "Xbox Music" in the music app, but in some places, such as on the debit you'll see on your credit card, you might see the "Zune" moniker (this may soon be gone altogether, however).

Find a song or album you want to buy, click or tap it to select it, and then click Buy Album or Buy Song. Your default payment method will appear, such as your credit card information. Click or tap Confirm to purchase your song or album.

Configure the Music App

The Music app can be configured in the same way as any other
Windows Store app: just access the Settings charm. You'll see the
following links:

- **Account**   The interface for managing account info is stylized a
  little differently from Windows 8 Settings panes in other apps
  and offers a lot of information. From here you can view your
  currently signed-in account, the status of that account, see your
  monthly plans, manage devices, redeem codes, and update
  billing or contact information.

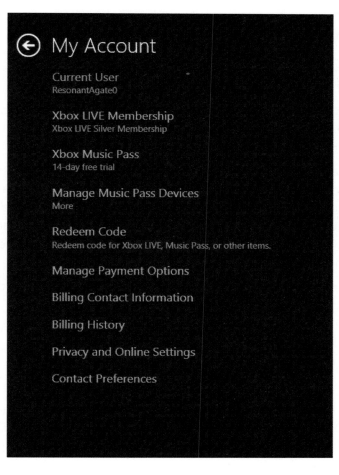

- **Preferences**   Choose here whether or not to go directly to the My Music screen—bypassing the main Xbox Music app when opening the app—whether to automatically retrieve album art and data, and whether to force the user to enter a password for every purchase.
- **About**   View information about the Music app here as well as privacy information.
- **Feedback**   Give Microsoft feedback about the Music app.
- **Permissions**   Decide whether to allow the Music app to notify you when you're elsewhere in Windows.
- **Rate & Review**   Rate and review the Music app in the Windows Store.

Explore the Video App

The Windows 8 Video app lets you play and manage your video, movie, and television programs in one place, as well as buy new videos. Here's how to fire up the Video app and get familiar with it:

1. Start the Video app by clicking or tapping its tile on the Start screen. If it's not there, right-click or press and hold on an empty part of the Start screen or swipe from the bottom or top edge toward the center of the screen. Then choose All Apps and start it from there. The Video app appears, as shown in Figure 10-2. The app starts on the Spotlight section.

2. Scroll or swipe left or right to see additional sections. From extreme left to right, the sections are as follows:

   - **My Videos**   Any videos that you've included in your Videos library or purchased will be here.
   - **Spotlight**   Videos of all types will be here based on what Microsoft wants to feature, and this section changes often.
   - **Movies Store**   Browse movies that are available for streaming or see movie trailers for upcoming movies.
   - **Television Store**   Browse popular television shows here.

Figure 10-2 *The Windows 8 Video app*

Play Videos

To play a video under My Videos, simply click or tap it and it will launch. To play other videos, you have to buy them first and then you can access them under My Videos. To see all of your available videos, click the My Videos link at the top of the section. You'll see any videos you have here, as shown in Figure 10-3. Four categories appear at the top of the page: All, Movies, TV, and Other.

 You can select from a drop-down list at the upper left to sort videos by Date Added or A to Z. The Movies and Television tabs give you different sorting options, such as sorting by release year for movies or viewing TV shows arranged by series.

Figure 10-3   *The My Videos screen*

 Smartphone videos will go under Other.

Right-click or swipe from the bottom or top edge toward the center of the screen to see a controls overlay. With this you can open the current file in the app's File Explorer, repeat it, pause or unpause play, play the file to another device, or go to the next or previous video.

Buy Videos

Buying videos is easy. Simply select a video you don't already have from the three sections on the Video app other than My Videos. The options you'll see, depend on whether you're selecting a movie or a TV series.

For movies, select one and you'll see Buy, Rent, Explore Movie, and Play Trailer. For a TV series, select one and you'll see View Seasons or

Explore Series. If you select a whole series, you'll see the Buy a Season Pass option, which will give you the entire series. If you select a single episode, you'll instead see the Buy Episode button.

Select a purchase button and your default payment method will appear, such as your credit card information (entering this information is discussed in Chapter 11). Click or tap Confirm to purchase or rent your video.

 When you buy the video, you'll often be given the choice between standard definition or high definition. The latter costs more.

Configure the Videos App

Configure the Videos app by accessing the Settings charm from the Charms. The options here are nearly identical to what I discuss in the "Configure the Music App" section earlier in this chapter. There is one less option on the Preferences pane, but other than that it's the same information and the same process to change it.

Configure Windows Media Player

Microsoft has changed a lot in Windows 8, but some familiar old apps work pretty much the same, and Windows Media Player is no exception. Because the Music and Video apps really replace Windows Media Player, I don't cover it in depth in this chapter. When you first start the software, you have to configure it, so I will walk you through that process and show you how to play a song and access your playlists.

1. Start Windows Media Player by tapping or clicking its tile. By default, you can find Windows Media Player on your All Apps screen.

2. Choose Recommended Settings or Custom Settings. The latter allows you to configure whether Windows Media Player can automatically download album art and data, whether to send player information to Microsoft, and other options.

3. Click Next. Choose whether to use Windows Media Player as the default media player for Windows or choose to select specific file types for Windows Media Player to be the default player for. Then click Finish. Windows Media Player appears, as shown in Figure 10-4, and imports your music and any data about your music from the Internet.

 If you choose Select All when associating file types, those files that the Music and Video apps are set to be the player for by default will have their icons replaced with Windows Media Player icons.

4. Select Music in the left menu to access your music files.

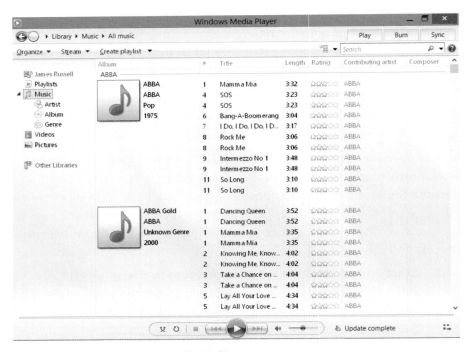

Figure 10-4 *Music in Windows Media Player*

5. Click or tap any field and then do so again—not as fast as a double-click or double-tap but faster than single clicks or taps—to edit information about a song. For example, you can click the stars to rate a song or change the name.

Some fields aren't editable. Try clicking one and you'll end up playing the song instead.

6. Click or tap the Organize menu in the upper left to find options—including the Options item—where you can configure Windows Media Player.

7. Select Videos from the menu at the left to access your video files. Double-click or double-tap a video to play it.

8. Select Pictures in the menu at left to view and manage your photos. You can right-click and choose Play to play the images in a slideshow.

9. Click Playlists in the left menu to access your playlists or create new ones.

Playlists can include images, videos, and music files. For example, if you put a picture, video, and song in the same playlist, Windows Media Player will open a window showing the image and then fade into the video followed by the song.

10. Click or tap the Burn tab in the upper right of the window to start burning a disc. Insert a blank disc and then drag items—be they videos, photos, or music—to the Burn pane to put them in the burn list. Click Start Burn to start the burn process.

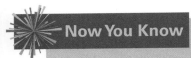 **Now You Know** **Media Center Doesn't Come with All Versions of Windows 8**

Windows Media Center wasn't available at the time this book was being written, so I wasn't able to write about it here. In the meantime, if you have Windows 8 Pro, you probably don't have Media Center by default and you can't play Blu-ray discs or even regular DVDs. Microsoft has essentially decoupled Media Center and expensive royalty-based software codecs from Windows 8 to help bring down the cost of the operating system for those people who don't watch movies on their computer and don't want to pay for functionality they don't need. If your version of Windows 8 doesn't include Media Center, you can get the Media Center Pack upgrade or the Windows Pro pack (depending on the version of Windows 8 you have) by choosing Add Features to Windows from the System and Security section of the Control Panel window. You will have to pay $9.99 for the upgrade, but you will then be able to use Media Center and play Blu-ray discs and DVDs.

11

Play Games on Windows 8

Windows 8 includes a whole new type of gaming interface based on the Windows 8–style touchscreen interface, and for the first time Microsoft is bringing Xbox and Windows together by releasing Xbox games and Xbox LIVE data and connectivity in Windows.

Most past versions of Windows came with at least *Solitaire*, *Minesweeper*, and other such games—but no longer. Windows 8 Pro doesn't include games by default, nor does it come with the Xbox tiles that come with consumer versions of Windows 8. At the launch of Windows 8, the Xbox Games app and Windows Store offer access to 40 Xbox-branded games for the Windows 8–style interface—including *Microsoft Solitaire Collection, Mahjong* and *Minesweeper*. So don't worry if you were a fan of those games; you can still get them for free via the Xbox Games app. More games are available from Windows Store.

In this chapter I'll show you how to download, install, and start playing probably the most popular Windows game of all: *Solitaire*. I'll also sum up a few of the better Windows 8–style and desktop games available at the time of this writing.

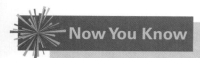

Log In to the Xbox Games App with Your Xbox LIVE ID

Logging in to your Windows 8 computer using your Xbox LIVE ID allows you to start your Windows 8 experience with your Xbox 360 data at your fingertips via the Games app on your Windows 8 device. You'll be able to earn trophies on Xbox LIVE games and share that data between your Xbox and Windows 8 PC, play games online with others, and keep your profile up to date right from Windows.

Explore the Xbox Games App

The Xbox Games app includes a lot of information. As is standard with Windows Store apps, the app is set up to scroll from left to right instead of up and down like desktop apps do. From the Start screen click or tap the green Games app with a white image of an Xbox controller on it to open the Xbox Games app. If it's not there, right-click or press and hold an empty part of the Start screen and choose All Apps to find it there.

When you open the Games app you'll see categories organized in large boxes from left to right, as is standard for a Windows Store app. Instead of starting at the extreme left like most other Windows Store apps, including Windows Store, the Xbox Games app starts you on the third section to the right: Spotlight. Scroll left and you'll see the first two sections, which are devoted specifically to your Xbox profile and friends, respectively.

The six categories on the Xbox Games app are as follows:

- **Profile box**   This section is unnamed, but it includes your Xbox LIVE avatar, if any, as well as your name, profile, achievements, motto, bio, and location information.

- **Friends**   See and interact with any friends you have on the Xbox LIVE network here.

- **Spotlight**   Games that Microsoft wants to call out to you are listed here. Some of them may be new, others may be advertisements for Microsoft's gaming partners or for Microsoft's own games. This list is dynamic and changes periodically.

- **Games Activity**   You won't see anything here until you play a game, or perhaps even a few of them. After that point you'll start seeing your game play statistics here for the various games you've played.

- **Windows Game Store**   Games made for the Windows 8–style interface are available here. Some are free while others cost money. You can play these games on a Windows 8 device or on your Xbox 360.

- **Xbox 360 Game Store**   Games you find here can only be played on an Xbox 360. Select games in this section to view demos, buy new games, or play games on your Xbox 360.

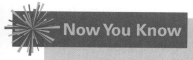 **Xbox Is Being Integrated into Windows 8**

If you have an Xbox LIVE account for your Xbox 360, you can log in to Windows 8 with this account. From there you can control your Xbox via your touchscreen Windows 8 device using the Xbox SmartGlass app, which you can find for free in the Windows Store. An Xbox 360 is required to use the app. A similar app is available for Windows Phone 8 so that you can use your phone to control your Xbox 360. Further, Microsoft is integrating Xbox LIVE achievements, badges, friends, and other features into the Windows 8 Xbox Games app, as well as Microsoft-made games such as those discussed in this chapter, to try and bring the Xbox 360 and Windows 8–style gaming interface together.

Get Games from the Xbox Games App

Because Microsoft is shifting its method of distributing apps to a central online store "buy once, run anywhere" model, you now have to go and get games from the Xbox Games app before it's on your system. You can then download it to any Windows 8 device you log in to.

Get *Microsoft Solitaire Collection*

Because *Solitaire* is such a popular Windows game—and because it no longer comes by default with all versions of Windows 8—I'll use the *Microsoft Solitaire Collection* game to show you how to get a game from the Xbox Games app. The next sections discuss the basics of playing and configuring the game.

1. Click or tap the Games tile on the Start screen. The Xbox Games app appears, as shown in Figure 11-1. Categories of apps in large boxes (made up of smaller tiles) show various individual apps that are being featured and in some cases ads.

2. Scroll or swipe right and click the Windows Game Store group. Click or tap the link with that exact text near the top of the screen.

3. Select a game, in this case *Microsoft Solitaire Collection*, by clicking or tapping its tile. Click or tap Install. Windows installs the new game and notifies you of such near the top right of the screen. When the app is installed, Windows notifies you via a toast notification and puts a tile for the new game on your Start screen. If you're installing a paid game, you'll have to pay for it before you see the Install button.

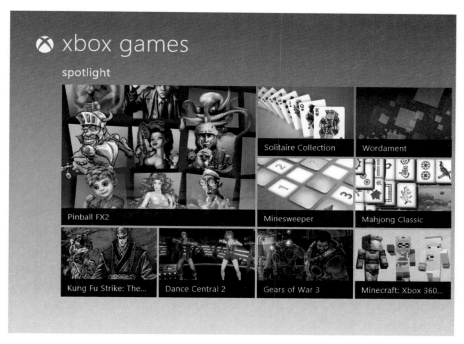

Figure 11-1   *The Xbox Games app*

 From the Start screen, right-click or press and hold on the new tile, which defaults to the Larger setting. Choose Smaller if you don't want it to have a double-wide tile.

Customize and Get Info About the Xbox Games App

The only Settings available under Preferences on the Settings charm for the app are the ability to turn on or off the requirement that you sign in before making purchases or managing your account. Other than the "Preferences" replacing "Game Info," the rest of the settings are the same as those described in the "Customize Game Settings" section later in this chapter.

Windows Store and Xbox Games Include Different Games

Not all games are accessible via the Xbox Games app. Games available via that app, at least as of the time of Windows 8's release, were reserved for Microsoft's games only. You can find other games in the Windows Store under the Games section interspersed with Microsoft games. The Windows Store is discussed in detail in Chapter 12.

Play *Microsoft Solitaire Collection*

Windows 8 is the focus of this book, not discussing how to play games. The new Windows 8–style game interface—used either with a keyboard and mouse or via a touchscreen device—*does* warrant coverage, however, so in the following sections I show you the basics of playing the game we downloaded in the earlier section, "Get *Microsoft Solitaire Collection*."

 If you or someone you're working with gets frustrated with the new touchscreen interface, playing around with this and other Windows games can help them get the hang of the Windows 8–style interface quickly and enjoyably.

Get Started Playing *Solitaire*

Without getting into the rules of the different types of *Solitaire* available in the *Microsoft Solitaire Collection*, playing the game is easy using either a mouse and keyboard or a touchscreen interface:

1. Start the *Solitaire* game from the Start screen.

2. Select Yes if you have an Xbox LIVE account to allow the game to access your Xbox LIVE data and information. Allowing this will let you be able to record trophies and statistics data.

3. Scroll or swipe to the right to see all of your options. As you can see in Figure 11-2, the list of types of *Solitaire* you can play is at the very left. To the right of that is your current theme, available themes, Awards, Leaderboard, Statistics, and How to Play instructions for each of the five types of *Solitaire* available.

Figure 11-2 *The* Microsoft Solitaire Collection *game*

4. Click or tap one of the five tiles at left to choose a type of *Solitaire* to play. For this example, I'll choose *Pyramid Solitaire*. The new game window appears, as shown in Figure 11-3. For your information, though, you have the following six options available:

- **Free Cell**   Use four free cells in the upper left to sort through multiple columns of cards and attempt to make series of cards in sequence to eventually sort by suit into the upper right of the window.

- **Klondike**   Uncover cards by moving cards onto other cards of a black suit for a red suit and a red suit for a card of a black suit that are one higher in value than the card itself. Eventually get all cards sorted by suit into the upper right corner.

Figure 11-3 *Pyramid Solitaire*

- **Pyramid**   Match two cards that together value 13 to uncover other cards in a pyramid fashion. Kings are worth 13 and can be removed alone. A queen plus a 1 card would also equal 13, as would a 10 and a 3 or a 7 and a 6, for example.

- **Spider**   Attempt to make series of cards to eventually sort by suit by moving cards from one pile to another. Spider is easily the most complex of the five solitaire games to understand.

- **TriPeaks**   Similar in look to *Pyramid Solitaire* but with three peaks instead of one, the goal of *TriPeaks Solitaire* is to tap a series of cards either one higher or one lower than the first card and remove cards from the table. The goal is to remove all cards from the table before you run out of cards in the deck.

- **Daily Challenges**   If you have an Xbox 360 connected to your PC you can play daily challenges of various types.

5. Click or tap your way through the initial rules or just select Close to skip them and start the game. You can click the Do Not Show Again check box so they won't reappear.

 Right-click or press and hold an empty part of the screen and select How to Play at any time to read about how to play the game.

6. To move cards with a mouse, click, drag, and drop cards with your left mouse button. For touchscreens, pick up a card by touching it with your fingertip, move it by dragging your fingertip to the desired location onscreen, and then drop it by removing your fingertip from the touchscreen.

 If you move a card into the wrong place, it'll move back to its original location and warn you why it did so. You can click the Do Not Show Again check box on these warnings and then choose Close to make the warnings go away, but you still won't be able to put cards in the wrong places.

Change the Game's Theme

On the game's main screen you'll see a Theme section to the right of the links to the games. Simply click or tap one of these themes to change the way the screen and cards look in your game. For example, the Western theme shows 1800s-style cards on a wooden surface, reminiscent of bars in the American Wild West, as shown in Figure 11-4.

Customize Game Settings

You can customize significant aspects of your game. Accessing game settings is similar to accessing settings for any Windows Store app.

Figure 11-4 TriPeaks Solitaire *in a Western theme*

While in the game interface, access the Settings charm and then Game Options. The key, though, is where you do so. Follow these steps to see what I mean:

1. Start the *Microsoft Solitaire Collection* app from the Start screen. If you're already in the app, get to the Home screen if you're not there already by clicking the Back button in the upper left corner of your screen.

   Access the Settings charm. The following links appear at the top of the pane:

   - **About**   Find the game's privacy information and credits.
   - **Game Options**   Access the various game options.

- **How to Play**   Get information on how to play the specific type of *Solitaire* you've opened.

- **Credits**   Select this link to see detailed game credits.

- **Permissions**   Allow the game to post notifications to Xbox LIVE.

- **Rate and Review**   Click this link to rate and review the game in the Windows Store.

2. Select Game Options. The Game Options pane appears with a fairly limited set of options that apply to all games, such as sound settings and whether to display hints, alerts, and the tutorial.

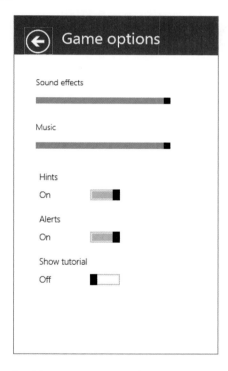

3. Go back to the Home screen and start a game of *Klondike Solitaire*, *Spider Solitaire*, or *Pyramid Solitaire*. For this example, I'll start a *Klondike Solitaire* game.

4. Access the Settings charm and then click or tap Game Options. The Game Options pane appears with more options on top of the ones you saw before, which are now below the game-specific options on the pane.

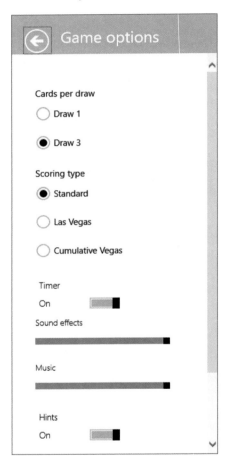

Which options you see depend on the game you're playing. Put simply, if you're in an actual game there are more options to be had based on that particular game. If you're on the Home screen, you only get the Settings that apply to all games. The preceding illustration shows options for *Klondike Solitaire*, which include changing the number of cards in each draw and changing the scoring type. *Pyramid Solitaire* has only a timer option to toggle, *Spider Solitaire* has only options to change the amount of suits, and the *TriPeaks Solitaire* and *Free Cell Solitaire* games have no game-specific options at all. It just depends on the game's rules.

Check Out Other Windows Games

While *Solitaire* is definitely a Windows staple, it's not the only game available. Windows 8 launched with 40 Xbox games available in the Xbox Games app and Windows Store, along with many other games. A few of the more noteworthy free games include the following:

- **Minesweeper** Right alongside *Solitaire* in Windows gaming history is *Minesweeper*, and it's free. The game has a new look but hasn't changed a bit in terms of game play. Achievements have been integrated just as they have been in all Xbox games from the Xbox Games app or Windows Store. For instance, blow up a bomb in your board to get the "It Happens to Everybody!" achievement.

- **Mahjong** In new, touchscreen-friendly versions, the old *Mahjong* tile game has been souped up with new graphics and animated puzzle backgrounds (see Figure 11-5). Playing is simple: Match two tiles to reveal more tiles and eventually uncover the board. Multiple *Mahjong* games are available via the Windows Store Games section, including *Microsoft Mahjong*, which is also available from the Xbox Games app in the Windows Games Store section and includes achievements integrated into Xbox LIVE, unlike the other versions.

- **Puzzle games** From *Rome Tetris* to *Tilt Maze*, *Ludo*, *Tic Tac Toe*, and *Hangman*, at the launch of Windows 8 at least a dozen puzzle games are available in the Windows Store.

- **Word games** Word games are huge on mobile devices today, and Windows 8 has enough word games to suit even the most voracious word game players—although as of the Windows 8 launch, the granddaddy of all word games—*Scrabble*—is not available as a Windows Store app as yet. A few of the word games available include Microsoft's *Wordament* app of Windows Phone fame, *Wordfeud*, *Word Search*, and *Wacky WordSearch Free*.

Figure 11-5 Microsoft Mahjong

Play Windows 8 Desktop Games

Windows has quite the legacy of games, for both computers and non-Windows RT devices. All of these games still work just fine with Windows 8, although working with them via a touchscreen might take some getting used to. There are too many games for the Windows 8 desktop to count, but some of the latest and greatest games work great with Windows 8. The following are a few of the more popular games as this book is being written:

- *Diablo III* Blizzard Entertainment's latest offering smashed sales records, selling 3 million copies in the first 24 hours and 6 million copies in its first week. The game is an action-adventure hack-and-slash game that received great reviews and has more than 10 million members. The game does require an Internet connection at all times, even for a single-player game, for digital rights-management purposes to help counter piracy.

- *World of Warcraft*   Although eight years old as of this writing, *WoW* is getting a bit long in the tooth in terms of massive multiplayer online roleplaying games (MMORPGs). Nevertheless, Blizzard Entertainment is still moving its franchise forward with the autumn 2012 release of *Mists of Pandaria* and the game still has a large community of dedicated players.

- *Star Wars: The Old Republic*   When LucasArts decided to move on from Sony Online Entertainment after that company's *Star Wars: Galaxies* game collapsed, they chose Bioware, the company that created *Star Wars: Knights of the Old Republic*, to create the next Star Wars–themed MMORPG. Now, more than five years in the making, *Star Wars: The Old Republic* is a reality—and a great game. Play on the side of the Sith or the Republic and level up your character while traveling around the Star Wars universe with other Star Wars fans.

- *Borderlands 2*   First-person shooter *Borderlands* by Gearbox Software was available on multiple platforms and is a much-loved space-themed role-playing game full of aliens, loot, and more aliens. The sequel to *Borderlands* has been highly anticipated for its improvement to game mechanics and online play, among other things.

12

Get Apps from
the Windows Store

Windows 8 brings apps for the operating system under a single store much like Apple does with iTunes App Store and Google does for its Android platform with Google Play. The result is Windows Store, which when tied to a Microsoft account allows you to download free and paid apps and have them forever be associated with that account. In this way you can easily download those apps to new devices simply by logging in with the same Microsoft account and downloading and installing the apps from the Windows Store.

In this chapter I show you around the Windows Store—show you how to buy, download, and install apps from it—and wrap up with a list of some of the more notable software in the Windows Store at the time of the Windows 8 launch, when this book was being finalized.

Browse the Windows Store

Windows Store is an app in itself that you use to browse through and find other apps that you want to download and install. The following sections show you how to find the apps you want by surfing through Windows Store's categories and how to download and install an app when you do find one you want.

Find Apps You Want

Start the Windows Store by clicking or tapping the green Store icon on the Start screen. You'll see the Spotlight section first, as shown in Figure 12-1.

 If you see a number on the Windows Store app tile, that means many of your apps have updates available. Enter the Windows Store and click the Updates link in the upper right of the screen to install your updates.

Scroll or swipe to the right to see more categories, of which there are quite a few. The following sections describe the Spotlight category and the others.

Notice in Figure 12-1 that each section has two potential subsections to the right in green boxes. At the top is Top Free, where you can see the top free apps, and below that is New Releases if there are any new releases in that category. Not all categories have both green boxes. If there are no free apps in a category, for example, there will be no Top Free box next to the category.

Figure 12-1 *The Windows Store Spotlight section*

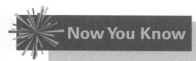 **Windows Store Will Grow**

Microsoft has already said that Windows Store is able to handle Intel-based apps and even apps that have Intel-based and RT-based versions for the same app. A few desktop apps are present already in the Windows Store, but you can't buy them from the Store yet. You can expect to eventually be able to buy Microsoft Office, Adobe Photoshop, and other Windows apps via the Windows Store as soon as Microsoft and software vendors work out agreements to make it happen. Expect some diversion from the typical "buy once, run anywhere" in these cases. More expensive Windows software has a certain number of seats per license and Windows Store will have to be able to respect more limited licensing options.

Spotlight

The Spotlight category is where Microsoft highlights certain apps from itself and its partners. As a result, the category really isn't one; you'll see apps from all categories under the Spotlight section, which changes periodically as Microsoft chooses to highlight new apps.

Games

Non-Xbox games are housed here. Although you'll find some Xbox games here as well, you will not find non-Xbox games in the Games app. See Chapter 11 for more information on the Games app and games available via the Windows Store.

Social

Although at the time of the Windows 8 launch there weren't a whole lot of apps in this category—such as Twitter, Facebook, or LinkedIn— Skype is there, as are third-party apps like Tweaker, which reads tweets to you, and Tweetro, which attempts to bring Twitter to the Windows 8– style interface.

Entertainment

Apps that are related to fun but that are not games are included here. Apps found here include Netflix, Hulu Plus, StumbleUpon, Xbox SmartGlass, and Cracked.com. While there weren't a lot of high-profile apps here at the launch of Windows 8, it is likely this category will get a lot of new apps fast.

Photo

The Windows 8 Photos app is fairly limited. If you want to stretch your photography skills further, check out some of the apps here. Although at the time of this writing major desktop apps such as the full version of Adobe Photoshop were not available yet, Adobe and Corel had managed to include a few desktop apps in the Windows Store, as you can see in Figure 12-2, such as Adobe Photoshop Lightroom 4.1 and Corel PaintShop Pro X4. You can't buy these apps from Windows Store, however. You have to go online to buy them.

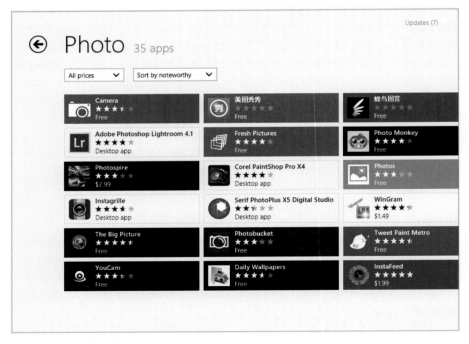

Figure 12-2   *The Photos section includes some desktop apps.*

Music & Video

Alongside the default Windows 8 Music and Video apps—which you can get here if you don't already have them—this section includes a few of the apps you might expect to see here, such as Slacker Radio, DVD-creation software, and a free guitar tuner.

Sports

Of course, the default Sports app is here, but beyond that there are NFL 2012, MotorSport, and the College Football Playbook. Many of the apps here may not interest you, such as New Zealand Cricket or ESPN Cricinfo, but keep your eye out for more official apps from the major sports networks themselves, such as MLB, NBA, and others.

 If you're looking for WWE wrestling, it's under Entertainment, not Sports.

Books & Reference

This section contains books and reference materials, including several copies of the Bible, an English-to-German dictionary, the periodic table, a Kindle reader, and a Wikipedia Windows Store app. Missing so far are ebook releases other than those for Kindle.

Now You Know **Faith-Related Apps Are Spread Out Everywhere**

So far, Microsoft hasn't included a Religion & Spirituality section, and it shows. Faith-related apps are there, but they're all over the place in the Windows Store. Multiple copies of the Bible are under Books & Reference, for example, but the Holy Qur'an is under Education and the Jewish Calendar and prayer apps are under Lifestyle.

News & Weather

Along with the default Weather and News apps, you'll find some big brands represented here, such as the *USA Today*, Weatherbug, and AccuWeather apps, an app for *The New York Times* and *Chicago Tribune* (expect to see more major newspapers following suit), and an Associated Press app. Missing so far are other major news sites like CNN and *The Huffington Post*.

Health & Fitness

As categories go, this one is pretty slim. Among the apps available here are two body-mass index (BMI) calculators, first aid apps, a sleep timer, a horoscope app, a baby monitor, and an acupressure treatment app.

Food & Dining

Here you'll mostly find cooking-related apps such as cookbooks, but also available are a My Wine Lists app, a cocktail app, and a video recipes app. Look forward in the future to apps from or related to big names in cooking like Rachael Ray or Gordon Ramsay. Food Network does have a paid app as of the time of this writing.

Lifestyle

Included in this category are apps similar to those in other categories; for example, you'll find a horoscope app here, too, in addition to the one in Health & Fitness. Also present are a Jewish Calendar, a Bible Verse a Day app, an Apartment Search app, and both, a free and a paid Craigslist app. The Oprah Winfrey Network has an app available as well.

Shopping

This is another section that doesn't have much in it yet. The only apps you're likely to recognize off the bat are eBay, Buy.com, Office Depot, Yellow Pages, and NewEgg. Expect in the future to see Amazon.com and other major shopping portals represented here.

Travel

Other than the default Travel app, there really isn't much here that isn't very localized, such as Stockholm Travel and Korea Bus Information. There is an app called The Tower by American Airlines, but it simply lets you look behind the scenes at six airports. SkyScanner helps you find cheap flights fast and XE Currency allows you to transfer foreign currency, even though other currency converters are in Finance, too.

Finance

Apps related to finances reside in this section, although at the time of this writing there just wasn't much here. Although XE Currency Converter is in Travel, more currency converters are here, as are multiple apps for stock management and quotes. Also noteworthy is a Checkbook HD application where you can import OFX files from your bank to manage your checking account via the Windows 8–style interface. So far the only bank represented here at the time of this writing is Bank of America, but that will likely change soon.

Productivity

Productivity is one of the most populated sections. The apps here are diverse and some are even desktop apps. Two apps are Windows 8 default apps, but you can also find Microsoft's Remote Desktop app, OneNote, EverNote, QuickNote, and Adobe Reader X.

 Microsoft Office 2010 is represented here, but you can't currently buy it from this section. You have to click the link to go to the Office.com Web site and buy the suite from there.

Tools

Related to productivity, the tools and utilities in this section let you perform common Windows operations in the Windows 8–style interface. In some cases, you have to pay for this luxury, such as with the telnet app, whereas other apps, like the IP Address or Ping apps, are free. The Google Search app is available here.

Security

As of this writing, there are not very many apps available and those that are here are desktop apps, for the most part. Other apps include a password generator and a locking application for Windows 8, and a password manager. Expect this section to explode as Windows 8 grows in popularity.

Business

Dubiously different from Productivity in scope, Box is the only big-name app in this section, and other than Splashtop Remote Desktop and PC Monitor there just isn't much here at Windows 8's launch.

Education

Filled as you might expect with apps for flash cards, mathematics, and other related items, this channel also has a few unexpected gems: the Holy Qur'an is here—instead of in Books & Reference with the Bible, strangely—and Star Chart, shown in Figure 12-3, which is one of the cooler Windows Store apps.

Figure 12-3   *The Star Chart app*

Government

This section is easily the leanest of the bunch. The potential for this section is huge, but right now it doesn't have much other than some county tax assessor apps, a paid White House app—there will likely be a free one eventually—and an app called Government Social that lets you follow your representatives in government as they microblog on Twitter.

Sort Store Apps

Enter any of the Windows Store's sections and you'll see drop-down list boxes near the top of the screen with which you can sort through the apps by price, rating, newness, or noteworthiness. Certain sections have different sorting features. The Games section, for example, has a list of subcategories that you can choose from to help narrow your search.

Search Windows Store

If you know the name of the app you're looking for and don't want to deal with finding it via surfing through the various and sundry sections in the Windows Store, simply search for it using the Search charm as follows:

1. Access the charms and select the Search charm. The Search pane appears.

2. Make sure Apps is selected in the pane at the right and type a search query into the text field at the top of the pane.

3. Select from your results, if any.

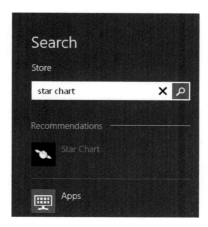

Set Up Your Payment Account

Before you can download any paid apps from Windows Store, you need to set up your billing information. Follow these steps to do so:

1. Open Windows Store and access the Settings charm.

2. Click or tap Account Info at the top of the Settings pane that appears. The Account Info page appears, as shown in Figure 12-4.

3. Click or tap the Add Payment Method button.

4. Type in your billing information. You can choose to use a credit card or PayPal.

5. Click or tap Submit when done.

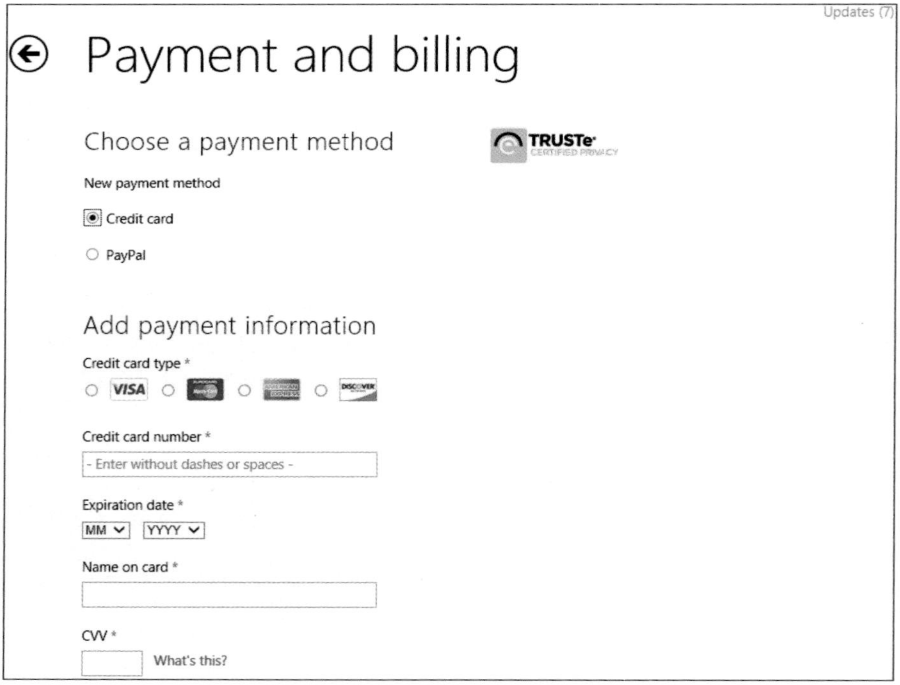

Updates (7)

← Payment and billing

Choose a payment method ![TRUSTe CERTIFIED PRIVACY]

New payment method

◉ Credit card

○ PayPal

Add payment information

Credit card type *

○ VISA   ○ MasterCard   ○ AMERICAN EXPRESS   ○ DISCOVER

Credit card number *

[- Enter without dashes or spaces -]

Expiration date *

[MM ▾] [YYYY ▾]

Name on card *

[   ]

CVV *

[   ] What's this?

Figure 12-4 *Add your billing information.*

Get and Buy Apps

Downloading and installing apps is easy, and is described in Chapter 11.
Buying apps is just an additional click or tap of a button. If you select
an app that costs money, you'll see a Buy button instead of an Install
button. If you click Buy, you'll have to confirm the purchase by selecting
the Confirm button.

 Once you do click Confirm, the transaction can't be canceled.

Sometimes, you'll also see a Try button; select it to try a trial version
of the app. The telnet app, for example, gives you a six-day trial of the
full app.

Configure Windows Store

Like any Windows Store app, you can
configure the app's settings easily from
the Settings pane. Follow these steps to
do so:

1. Access the Settings charm from
   the Windows Store main page.
   The Settings pane will appear
   with several app-specific options
   at the top:

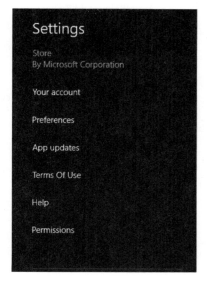

Settings

Store
By Microsoft Corporation

Your account

Preferences

App updates

Terms Of Use

Help

Permissions

- **Your Account**   Switch your user account, add or edit payment information, or choose to remove computers from your account. Near the bottom of the screen you'll see the various computers attached to your account. Click these to remove them at will. You can put an app you get from the Windows Store on up to five computers. You can also toggle whether or not Windows 8 prompts you for your password every time you make a purchase or not.

You can only add a computer by logging in to it and installing an app on it using your username.

- **Preferences**   Only two settings are here, both of which are off by default and allow you to make it easier to find foreign language apps and accessibility apps.

- **App Updates**   Access this item to check for app updates and choose whether or not to install app updates automatically.

- **Terms of Use**   Read the terms of use for the Windows Store.

- **Help**   Access the Windows Store help documentation.

- **Permissions**   As with other apps, the only setting here is whether to allow the app to notify you of new updates and so on.

2. Select an option to change related information. There is no need to save changes. Windows 8 automatically saves changes as you make them.

Part III
Get Productive with Windows 8

13

Print Files and Manage Devices

Since the early days of personal computing, external devices—and in particular printers—have played a key role in personal computing. With the proliferation in the last several decades of other devices such as external hard drives, Webcams, cameras, flash drives, and smartphones, the PC has become sort of a hub for all kinds of devices. Windows 8 makes setting up external devices easy and intuitive. In this chapter you'll learn how to configure printers and USB, Bluetooth, and wireless devices, as well as how to print from desktop apps.

Set Up a Printer or Device

Most new printers and devices by major manufacturers are supported inherently by Windows 8 and will set themselves up after you plug a USB cord into your computer. Windows displays a notification telling you so.

If Windows fails to recognize and set up your computer automatically, you will have to set up the device manually. You can do so via the Control Panel or the Devices item in the Windows 8 PC Settings app, which is significantly easier to find and use, but you can (and may have to) use the tried-and-true Control Panel to do so. The following sections describe both processes.

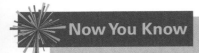

**Configuring Printers
in the PC Settings App Is Easier**

Configuring a printer in the PC Settings app is easier—if it works.
At the outset of Windows 8 at least, the functionality of the PC
Settings app didn't match that in the desktop interface. If your
printer cannot be configured via the PC Settings app, Windows will
tell you it didn't find your device and you'll have to manually set up
the device via the Control Panel.

Add a Printer or Device via PC Settings

The PC Settings app lets you easily add and configure your devices.
Unfortunately, if the device must be set up manually you will have to
do so via the Control Panel, as described in the next section. Most
modern hardware can be set up this way, however. Here's how to add
your device through the PC Settings app:

1. Access the charms and select Settings.

2. Select Change PC Settings at the bottom of the Settings pane.

3. Plug your printer or device into the computer via a USB or
   other cable or turn it on if it's wireless. For Bluetooth devices,
   make sure the device is broadcasting Bluetooth and that it's in
   pairing mode.

4. Select Devices and then Add a Device. Windows searches for
   your printer or device. If Windows finds your printer or device,
   select first its name and then choose Connect.

5. If the device is Bluetooth, Windows will display a code onscreen
   for you to enter into the device to pair it. Enter that code into
   the device to pair the device with your PC.

If you can't set up your device after following these steps, you'll
have to resort to the Control Panel to do so, as described in the
next section.

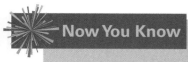

Now You Know **Bluetooth Devices Need to Be Paired**

Bluetooth is a wireless technology that uses radio waves to transmit voice and data over distances of up to about 160 feet. To protect your privacy, Bluetooth devices don't just automatically connect to one another; you first have to set both devices as discoverable and then pair them by getting a code from one device and inputting it into the other. Each Bluetooth device has a different pairing system, so I can't possibly cover the interfaces for all devices here, but as an example here's the method I used to pair my Nexus S phone running Android 4.0.4 (Ice Cream Sandwich) with my Windows 8 device:

1. On the Windows 8 device, access the charms and select Settings.

2. Select Change PC Settings at the bottom of the Settings pane and then click or tap Devices at the left of the window.

3. On the phone, tap Menu while on a home page and then tap System Settings.

4. Tap Bluetooth to turn it to the On setting if necessary and then click the name "Bluetooth" to open the Bluetooth settings.

5. Tap "Nexus S – Only Visible to Paired Devices" so it instead says "Nexus S – Visible to All Nearby Bluetooth Devices."

6. On the Windows 8 device, tap Add Device. The Nexus S is discovered. Click or tap Connect; Windows then displays a numeric code.

7. On the phone, a window pops up asking for the code you just got. Type it in and tap OK to pair the devices.

Add a Printer or Device via the Control Panel

The Control Panel hasn't changed much from Windows 7, and accessing your printers and devices should be a somewhat familiar process if you've used the Control Panel before:

1. Access the Control Panel, select Hardware and Sound, and then choose Devices and Printers.

2. Plug your printer or device into the computer or turn it on if it's wireless. For Bluetooth devices, make sure the device is broadcasting Bluetooth and that it's in pairing mode.

3. Select the Add a Printer or Add a Device button in the upper left of the window. Windows will search for devices.

4. If Windows finds your printer or device, select its name and then choose Next. If Windows doesn't find your printer or device, it will tell you so and you'll have to select Next to use other options to find the printer.

5. If Windows did not find your device, choose your method of setting up the printer from the resulting dialog box, as shown in Figure 13-1. You can choose to add a device by manually inputting a network name, TCP/IP network address, Bluetooth, or other wireless method.

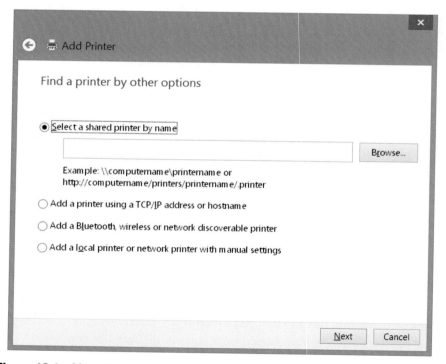

Figure 13-1   *Manually add a device.*

6. Select the appropriate radio button and then type in the required information depending on the option you choose. If the device is Bluetooth, choose that radio button. Click Next.

7. If the device is Bluetooth, Windows will display a code on your screen to enter into the device to pair it. Enter that code into the device to pair the device with your PC.

 If no methods described here work, such as might happen with very old printers or those that aren't functioning properly, see the manual or online documentation for your device and contact the hardware vendor if necessary.

Set a Default Printer

You should set your default printer as the printer you use most often to minimize the amount of clicking or tapping you have to do to print a typical document. Windows 8 includes "devices" in the Printers section that really aren't actual printers, as shown in Figure 13-2. You can see "Microsoft XPS Writer" as well as "Fax." These appear regardless of whether you have a fax machine or not, and whether or not you use Microsoft's XPS Writer. Microsoft XPS Writer may even be listed as your default printer, or you may have more than one printer for various functions. Your default printer will have a green check mark over its icon, as you can see in Figure 13-2.

You can easily change your default printer. Here's how:

1. Open the Control Panel, select Hardware and Sound, and then select Devices and Printers.

2. Right-click or press and hold the image of the printer you want to set as the default and choose Set as Default Printer from the context menu.

Figure 13-2 *Devices and printers in the Control Panel*

 **Now You Know**

The XPS Writer Is Microsoft's Version of PDF

Microsoft's XPS Writer allows you to create documents that will look the same in print as they do on screen—just as with PDF documents. Microsoft developed the XPS format using XML, and the format is an industry standard. Sending files to the XPS Writer as if it were a printer will give you an electronic document that cannot be altered. So, as you can see, XPS Writer really isn't a printer, you don't get a hard copy, but you can obviously print the XPS document on a real printer if you do need a hard copy.

Remove a Printer or Device

There are times when you have to remove a printer or device, such as when removing a flash drive, if you replace your printer, or if your printer or other device stops working and you need to reinstall it. Here's how to remove an installed device:

1. Open the Control Panel.

2. Select Hardware and Sound and then Devices and Printers.

3. Right-click or press and hold the icon for the printer you want to remove and choose Remove Device from the context menu.

4. Select Yes when Windows asks if you're sure you want to remove the device.

5. Remove any cables—for instance, if your printer is connected via a USB cord—and physically disconnect the device from the PC if necessary.

 When removing a USB device such as a flash drive or USB printer cable, make sure to click the Safely Remove Hardware and Eject Media icon in the system tray first.

Troubleshoot Devices with Device Manager

If you're having trouble using or accessing your devices, you can troubleshoot the problem first in Device Manager. Here's how:

1. Access the charms and select Search.

2. Type in "Device Manager," select Settings in the pane at right, and choose the Device Manager tile.

3. Find the device you're having problems with under the categories at the left side of the screen. For example, if you're having problems with your printer, click the Printers menu at left. If you can't use your device, chances are it will have a yellow exclamation mark over it, showing you that the device has issues.

4. Right-click or press and hold on the icon for the device and choose Update Driver Software from the context menu that appears to attempt to get new drivers for the device.

5. If reinstalling drivers doesn't work, right-click or press and hold on the icon for the device, choose Uninstall, and then see the earlier sections of this chapter to reinstall the device.

> If the preceding process doesn't work, you'll have to research the device on the Internet, initially at the manufacturer's site, and afterward possibly contact the device manufacturer for further assistance.

Printing in Windows 8 involves a new twist on previous versions of Windows: printing from Windows Store apps is quite different than printing from desktop apps. Printing from desktop apps, though, is pretty similar to printing in previous versions of Windows. To show the difference between Windows Store apps and Desktop apps, the following two sections describe printing in the Internet Explorer Windows 8–style app and then in the Internet Explorer desktop app. As you will see, the two processes are quite different.

Print Files in Windows 8 Mode

Printing files in Windows 8 mode is done using the Devices charm. Here's how to print from the Internet Explorer Windows Store app:

> Printing from a Windows 8–style app gives you far less control over your printout than you get when printing from a desktop app.

1. Open the Internet Explorer Windows 8–style app and surf to a page you want to print.

2. Access the charms and select Devices.

Figure 13-3 *The printer pane*

3. Choose your printer. Click More if you don't see it immediately. A pane slides in from the right named after your printer at the top, as shown in Figure 13-3. Here you can see a small preview of the printout, choose the number of copies, and change page orientation.

4. Click Print if you want to print, or click More Options to see what options are available for your printer. These options differ dramatically depending on your printer; Figure 13-4 shows the options for an HP Deskjet F4100. As you can see, there are a few options here, such as Duplex Printing, Collation, Pages Per Sheet, and various options for paper.

Figure 13-4 *Print options for an HP Deskjet F4100 printer*

You Give Up Some Control When Printing from Windows Store Apps

The Windows 8 experience is supposed to significantly simplify using Windows—and it does. This has a downside though. As you can see if you assess both processes, printing from desktop apps gives you far more control over your Web page printouts than Windows 8–style apps do. In Windows 8–style apps, printing from a Web page, for example, prints "Page 1 of 2" on the page whether you like it or not and you cannot print the URL or any other information on the page as you can in desktop Internet Explorer. As is evident in Microsoft's Windows 8 versions and pricing, versions of Windows 8 that include support for the Windows 7–compatible desktop apps (Windows RT does not) cost more because desktop apps in general give you more control over everything—including printouts—than their Windows 8–style counterparts so far do.

Print Files on the Desktop

Printing files from desktop apps is a process that differs somewhat depending on your printer and the app you're printing from, but many steps are the same regardless of your printer. In this section I discuss printing from desktop apps using the desktop version of Internet Explorer 10.

Printing a Web page in desktop mode is a familiar process if you've ever printed in a previous version of Windows. The following sections show you how to set up your page before printing, preview your printout, and print your document in Internet Explorer.

Adjust Page Setup to Print Only the Details You Want

In the desktop version of Internet Explorer, you can adjust the page setup for your printout so that only the details you want—if any—are printed with the page. If you have printed a Web page in the past, you may recall that by default Web pages are formatted with additional information that you may or may not want on your printouts. Here's how to adjust what prints on a page and what doesn't:

1. Access the gear wheel icon in the upper right region of the Internet Explorer window and choose Page Setup from the Print menu. The Page Setup window appears, as shown in Figure 13-5.

 **Now You Know** **Print Files from File Explorer**

You don't even need to open an application to print a file. To print a file from File Explorer, follow these steps:

1. Open File Explorer and navigate to the file you want to print.

2. Right-click or press and hold on the icon for the file you want to print and then select Print from the context menu that appears.

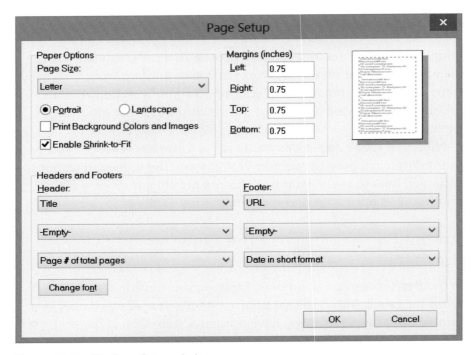

Figure 13-5   *The Page Setup window*

2. Configure your options as desired. The window includes three major sections with options under each:

   ● **Paper Options**   Choose paper orientation, paper size, whether to print background images, and whether to enable Shrink to Fit so the whole page fits on the printed portion of the paper.

 If you deselect Shrink to Fit, you may find your printouts cutting off the right side of the page.

   ● **Margins**   You can manually enter margin settings for each of the four sides of the page. The default value for all four is .75 inches.

- **Headers and Footers** This item has two items beneath it: one on the left for header information and one on the right for footer information. Use the drop-down menus to choose which information, if any, you want displayed in the headers and footers of your printed document. For example, if the page is your own page, you know the URL, so why have it displayed? Simply choose the drop-down menu and select Empty so it won't be displayed.

 You actually have a lot of options to choose from in terms of information you can display. Scroll through these drop-down menus and check out the various options. For example, one option lets you display the title of the page and another lets you display the time the page was accessed.

3. Select the Change Font button at the bottom of the window to change the font if desired.

4. Commit your changes by choosing OK.

Preview Your Printout

Before printing a page, you may want to preview the printout to make sure it's formatted the way you wish. Here's how to preview a Web page printout before printing it:

1. Access the gear wheel icon in the upper right region of the Internet Explorer window and choose Print Preview from the Print menu. The Print Preview dialog box appears, as shown in Figure 13-6.

2. Choose options across the top of the window as desired. The buttons in the upper left of the window let you print, change to Portrait or Landscape orientation, summon the Page Setup dialog box that's described in the previous section, show or hide header and footer information, print at a larger or smaller percentage than the actual page, or change your view of the page. If multiple pages are to be printed, you can navigate through them with the First, Previous, Next, and Last arrow buttons at the bottom of the window.

Figure 13-6   *The Print Preview dialog box*

3. Select the Print button in the very upper-left of the window
   to summon the Print dialog box and skip to Step 3 in the next
   section.

Print a Web Page

Printing a Web page in desktop mode is similar to that in previous
versions of Windows. Typically, you open a file, choose File, select Print,
configure your printout, and click the Print button. Here's how to print
in the desktop version of Internet Explorer:

1. Start Internet Explorer and surf to a page or file you want to print.

2. Access the gear wheel icon in the upper right region of the
   Internet Explorer window and choose Print from the Print menu.
   The Print dialog box appears, as shown in Figure 13-7.

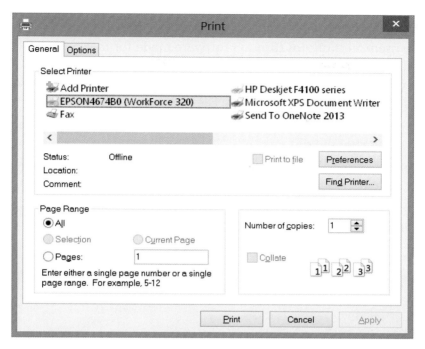

Figure 13-7   *The Print dialog box*

3. Select a printer if the default is not what you want to use, choose the number of copies to print, the page range to print, the collate options, and whether to print to a file (which you can do using Microsoft XPS Document Writer as your printer).

4. Select the Preferences button to view the preferences for your particular printer. This window will vary considerably depending on your printer.

5. Select the Options tab to view options for printing Web pages, including whether to print all frames separately (if frames aren't used, these options are grayed out) and whether to print a table of links and all documents linked to in the current document. Select Print.

Print Photos

Many users print photos through software made for that purpose. If you don't have such software, though, you don't need it. Windows 8 lets you print photos right from File Explorer. There are two main ways to print photos in Windows 8 from File Explorer:

- Right-click or press and hold on the image's thumbnail or item and choose Print.

- Select the file and then click or tap the Print button on the File Explorer Share tab.

Whichever option you choose, the Print Pictures dialog box appears, as shown in Figure 13-8.

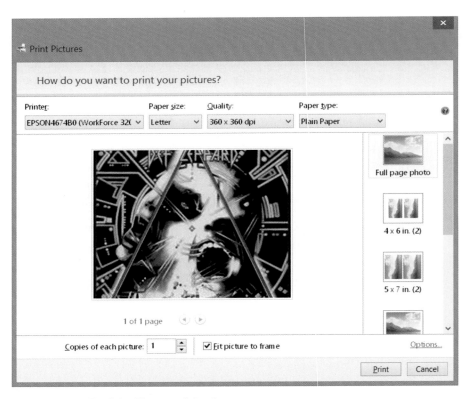

Figure 13-8   *The Print Pictures dialog box*

As you can see, Windows gives you quite a few options for printing your pictures:

- **Printer**   Choose which printer you want to use, or choose Microsoft XPS Document Writer, Fax, or Install A Printer.
- **Paper Size**   Choose the size of your paper.
- **Quality**   Choose the dots per inch (dpi) that you wish the photo to print at.
- **Paper Type**   Choose from many types of paper.
- **Print Layout**   Choose a layout for your printed photos. Many are listed, from a full-page image to a contact sheet.
- **Number of Copies**   Choose how many copies of the image to print.
- **Fit Picture to Frame**   Increase or decrease the size of the image to fit the page.
- **Options**   Choose whether to sharpen images for printing and whether to hide options that are not available for your chosen printer.

Simply click Print to print the photo once you're done choosing options.

14

Get Started with Microsoft Office

M icrosoft Office is inarguably a killer app, given that Office is a
staple of Windows PCs and has been for more than a decade. In
particular, Word, Excel, and PowerPoint have been used in grade
schools, universities, for home use, and in the business world more
than any other office productivity applications since before the turn
of the last century. Outlook and the Exchange server that powers it
has been—and still is—one of the most popular e-mail programs in
business communication.

Office 2013 is Microsoft's latest and greatest version of Office yet,
and its interface has been totally redesigned to match and integrate
the new Windows 8 interface and cloud networking features, such as
Sync. Newer applications in the Office suite—most notably OneNote,
which is a killer app itself—show amazing promise for integrating
different media and reshaping what people see as "documents."

With Windows 8 and Office 2013, Microsoft has broken step with
previous update cycles and revised Windows and Office simultaneously.
They did so for a very good reason: to overhaul both products to
include sharing and cloud computing. Setting up Office 2013 and using
Office apps in general has changed in dramatic fashion from Office
2010 and previous versions, and working with files is a redesigned
process that now includes cloud integration of Microsoft's SkyDrive.

Office for Windows RT Has a Limited Feature Set

ARM-based Windows RT tablets such as Microsoft's Surface RT come preinstalled with the "core four" Office apps—namely Word, Excel, OneNote, and PowerPoint—with a limited desktop mode that is not compatible with any Intel-based Windows software. Office for Windows RT is different than Office 2013 for Windows 8 in that it has no support for macros at all. If you want the full breadth of Office 2013 macros and VBA support, you need Windows 8, not Windows RT.

Because this is a Windows 8 book, I focus in this chapter on how to set up and sign into Office apps in general using Windows 8 instead of how to use individual Office apps themselves, which really haven't changed that much when you actually start working with them. Having said this, there are some very cool new features that I discuss at end of the chapter, along with a brief discussion of Microsoft's subscription service for Office 2013: Office 365.

 Office 2013 was in beta at the time this book was written, so version information and pricing was not yet available. The book was written using the public preview of Office 2013. Because of this, the final version may look and behave differently than the beta versions.

Set Up an Outlook.com Address

In addition to overhauling the company's flagship products Office and Windows, Microsoft is also taking the name from its popular Outlook mail software and creating a new Web-based e-mail service with it that is similar in scope to Google's Gmail. New @Outlook.com addresses can supplement or replace existing @MSN.com, @Hotmail.com, or @Live.com accounts. Microsoft has even gone so far as to let you transform an existing Microsoft e-mail account into a new Outlook.com account and—with your permission—delete the old account, although e-mails to that account will still come in to your Outlook.com account online. After you create a new Outlook.com address, you can use it to log into both Windows 8 and Office, which gets you a Web-based e-mail with a killer interface to boot.

Now You Know   Why Another Microsoft E-mail Domain?

Microsoft has a history with e-mail after acquiring Hotmail years ago, creating @MSN.com addresses to promote MSN.com years later, and @Live.com to accompany Xbox LIVE. So why another new Microsoft e-mail domain?

Outlook is a much-used and relied-upon communication application in the business world, and because of this reputation, people see Outlook as a secure Microsoft product—unlike with Hotmail, which has had some huge security guffaws in its history under Microsoft. Because having a Microsoft account is so critical to using Windows 8 and Office 2013 to their fullest potential with features such as Sync and SkyDrive, and making sure that Windows 8 and Office 2013 customers are kept very happy, the company knows that they need secure, free e-mail addresses available for users to create a Microsoft account if they don't already have one. Outlook. com solves the reputation problems Hotmail has accrued, delivers an intuitive and uncluttered interface that matches the Windows 8 Mail app, and further proves its productivity heritage implied by the Outlook name—as well as competes with Google Docs and Google Drive—by giving you free built-in access to Word, Excel, and PowerPoint Web apps *and* 7GB of SkyDrive cloud storage with your new Outlook.com account. Not a bad deal.

The following sections show you how to get a new Outlook.com account, transform an existing account into an Outlook.com account, and delete the previous account.

Upgrade an Existing Microsoft Account

If you already have a Microsoft account via another Microsoft e-mail service, you can upgrade that account to an Outlook.com account and even rename the account. Here's how:

1. Go to Live.com and log in with an existing Hotmail, Live.com, or MSN.com e-mail.

2. Select Options and choose Upgrade to Outlook.com and then click or tap Upgrade to Outlook. You will be taken to a new Outlook.com inbox.

3. Click the gear cog in the upper right corner and choose More Mail Settings.

4. Select Rename Your E-mail Address link. Type a desired name in the New Microsoft Account field and then Choose Outlook.com from the drop-down list (or Live.com or Hotmail.com if you want to rename to those). Click Submit. Microsoft changes the account and logs you out.

5. Use your new e-mail and password to log in. You are taken to your inbox, but Windows asks if you want any e-mail sent to your previous e-mail address in its own folder or if it should all go straight to the inbox. Choose either the A New Folder (you can rename it) option or the Inbox option and click Done.

 After renaming your Microsoft account, you'll have to change your Windows 8 user account (as described in Chapter 5) and switch to your new account in Office 2013. You can do this by clicking the little arrow next to your name in the upper right corner of any Office app window and selecting Switch Account.

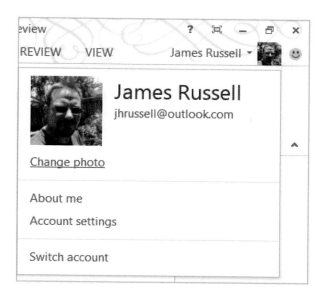

Get a New Outlook.com Address

You can get an Outlook.com e-mail address by visiting Outlook.com and signing up for an account using Microsoft's Web interface. Here's how:

1. Go to Outlook.com and click Sign Up.

2. Enter your information in the appropriate fields, such as your age, gender, desired account name, alternate e-mail address, phone contact information, or a security question.

3. Type in the CAPTCHA code at the bottom of the screen to prove you're not a robot and then click Submit. As long as the account name you wanted is available and you listed all of the required information, you'll be redirected to your new inbox. If not, correct whatever information you need to (the page will tell you in orange text if something's wrong) and try again.

Get Office 2013

If you have a new PC, you may have Office 2013 pre-installed. If not, you can purchase Office from a retail store or buy it online from Office. Microsoft.com. Microsoft offers a free trial of the software, so if you wish, you can try it for a few weeks and buy it before the trial expires. At the time of this writing, Office 2013 wasn't available yet, so I couldn't include a direct link in the book. However, Googling "Microsoft Office Trial" should get you there. Make sure whatever site you choose is a Microsoft.com site. Because this book is about Windows 8, I don't have room to show you how to install Office 2013, but the suite can be installed over the Internet and includes a pain-free installation process.

 Even if you don't buy the trial, you can keep Office on your computer to be able to view, but not edit, Office files.

Figure Out Which Office You Need

Before committing to buying Office 2013, make sure you get the right version. While versioning wasn't available at the time of this writing for Office 2013, Microsoft historically has a Home and Student edition available. You can use the Home and Student version of Office if you are a student or using the software for personal, non-commercial purposes—and you should if you can, because that version of Office is significantly cheaper than professional versions specifically because it is for personal use. However, the End User License Agreement of Microsoft Office Home and Student explicitly specifies that users cannot use it for commercial purposes. Writing a book and hoping to get paid? That's a commercial purpose. Using Office in a business—whether for profit or not? That's another commercial purpose.

If you're using Office in a business setting of any kind, you'll have to get a commercial version of Office.

 Keep your eye on this book's Google+ page or its Facebook page for more up-to-date information at https://plus.google.com/u/0/s/Windows%208%20Kickstart or http://www.facebook.com/Windows8Kickstart.

Buy Individual Office Programs

You can buy individual Office apps if you only want one or two programs from it and do not want to pay for the entire suite. This is especially true when you need a commercial, professional version of Office, because unlike the Home and Student version of Office, the professional versions are significantly more expensive than the Home and Student version. Luckily, if you want to use an Office program for commercial purposes but don't want to pony up for the whole suite, you don't have to. Don't want Excel? Don't buy it.

Buying individual programs isn't exactly inexpensive either, but if you do so you can pick and choose which applications you want to pay for—and when. For example, your author paid $133 for a two-PC transferable license to Microsoft Word 2010 (he also paid an extra $15 for a DVD copy of the software) to write this book rather than buy the whole suite. He intends to buy OneNote later and possibly Excel, but he has the *option* to wait. He didn't need Excel for this book, just Word, and so he just bought Word. Note that this is just an example. Pricing and options may well be different for Word 2013 and other Office 2013 apps, which by the time you read this book will likely have replaced their 2010 counterparts.

Configure Office 2013

When you first start an Office application—any application—the software will prompt you to sign into Office. Signing in replaces the process of the old "profile" in earlier versions of Office that consisted solely of your name and initials for your "signature" on comments or changes you make to a document. Signing into Office 2013, by contrast, is now like signing into Windows 8 and allows you to sync your settings and documents using your Windows SkyDrive. Just like with Windows 8, syncing your settings allows them to follow you from device to device.

 You only have to go through this process the first time you start an Office application.

I'll use Word as an application here, but the process is virtually identical no matter what program you use. Here's how to set up Office using Word:

1. Open Word 2013 from All Apps, which is accessible by right-clicking or pressing and holding on a blank section of the Start screen and selecting the All Apps button.

2. Click or tap Accept when the software asks you to accept the terms of use.

3. Word prompts you to sign in. Select Sign In to do so. If the program doesn't prompt you, just select the Sign In to Office link in the upper right corner of the window. A dialog box appears, as shown in Figure 14-1. Input your e-mail account and password and click OK to sign in. After doing so, you'll see both your Windows account profile picture and your name in the upper right corner of the Office applications.

 Sign in to Office with the same e-mail that you use for Windows 8 for seamless syncing of your Windows 8 and Office 2013 settings across devices.

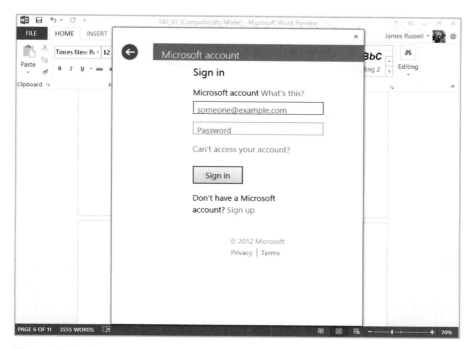

Figure 14-1 *Input your e-mail account and password.*

4. Office asks how you want the software to look. Choose an item from the drop-down menu if you want a subtle pattern in the ribbon at the top of your Office apps, or leave the default setting as None if you don't want a design. You can preview each style by selecting it and watching how the window pattern changes. You can always change it later in any Office program's Options.

The screenshots for this chapter were taken using the Calligraphy style.

5. Click or tap Next to view an image and text about SkyDrive. Select Next, watch the welcome video, select Next again, and then select All Done.

Manage Documents with Office 2013

Saving and opening documents in particular has been dramatically reimagined for Office 2013 because of SkyDrive. Specifically, there is now an extra step in opening documents when you have a SkyDrive set up (as discussed in Chapter 11). In the following sections, I'll show you how to open your documents from SkyDrive or your computer and how to add another location to store files on. The process may be somewhat different for other Office 2013 apps, such as OneNote, but the basics for Word, Excel, and PowerPoint (in particular) are very similar.

Open a Document

You can open a document in an Office app easily, but doing so is a little different than it was in previous versions of Office. Here's how to open a document in Word:

1. Open Word 2013 and click Open Other Documents at left. You can choose to open documents directly from the Recent Documents menu, but you likely won't have any recent document history unless you're upgrading a previous Office installation.

2. Select the File tab and then Open from the blue menu at left.

3. Choose a location to open a document from the Places section. If you choose SkyDrive or Computer, you will then have to click the large Browse icon to the right of the Places section, as shown in Figure 14-2. You can also choose Add a Place. This feature is discussed in the "Add a Location for Documents" section later in this chapter.

 After you have used the program to open a file or two, you will see shortcuts above the Browse icon to your current and recent folders.

4. Use the file browser window to browse to the folder your file is in and click or tap Open.

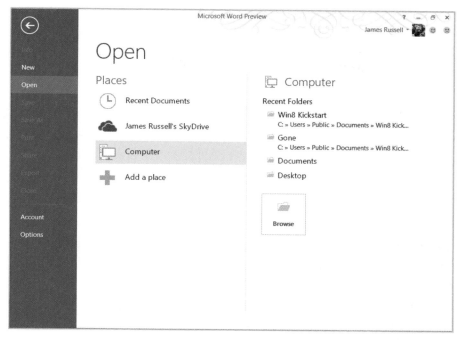

Figure 14-2 *Open a file from your computer.*

Save a Document

Saving a document is different from previous versions of Office in much the same way as opening a document is. Here's how to do it:

1. With an open document in Word, click or tap the File tab.

2. Click Save As the first time you save given document.

3. Choose a location to save the file under Places. If you click Computer or SkyDrive, you will then have to click the Browse icon.

 After you have used the program to edit and save a file or two, you will see shortcuts above the Browse icon to your current and recent folders.

4. Browse to the location you want the document saved, type in a name for the document, choose a file type if necessary, and click or tap Save. To save the file again later in its current location, you need only select the File tab and choose Save.

Add a Location for Documents

You can add a location to save documents to, such as a SkyDrive (if it hasn't been added already), an additional SkyDrive account, or an Office 365 SharePoint account. Here's how to add a location to save to:

1. Select the File tab from an open Word window and click Open.

2. Select Add a Place under the Places section.

3. Choose SkyDrive or Office 365 SharePoint. A window appears asking for your login credentials. Type them in and select Sign In. The account will appear under Places from now on.

Kickstart Office 2013 Apps

Although I don't have room to discuss Office 2013 individual apps and their features in depth, I did want to highlight some of the features that really complement the Windows 8 user experience as a whole. The following sections give you a brief rundown on some of the more powerful new features of the four core Office apps. Some of the more dramatic new features for Office 2013 include

- **A new look**   A Windows 8–style user interface has been applied to Office 2013 to make it match Windows 8's new desktop look, which removes distracting colors, gradients, and three-dimensional effects to help you focus on what you're doing. Only the active tab in an Office app has colored text, for example. Every tool not being used fades into the background. Only the File tab is actually a dark color; the entire rest of the ribbon now tries and succeeds pretty well in being as non-distracting as possible.

- **Improved graphics rendering**   With Windows 8, Microsoft has brought ActiveX, which used to be just for gaming, to bear on the entire Windows 8 and Office 2013 interface—and it shows.

Scrolling through documents, moving text and other items, and zooming in or out on a document is a more streamlined experience than in previous versions of Office.

- **Design tab**   The Office ribbon remains largely the same in Office 2013, with one key addition: design-related utilities and features have been moved to a new Design tab. Word, for example, includes themes, watermarks, and page color and border settings on the Design tab.

- **Auto-calculation of table data in Excel**   Excel now allows you to select a table's cells to instantly see the data calculations from that data.

- **Read mode**   In Word and PowerPoint, you can now access a reading view that lets you swipe through your document or presentation like an e-book, flipping pages by swiping left and right on your touchscreen device.

- **Skype**   Skype, owned now by Microsoft, will be integrated with Office 2013 by the time the software is finalized to give you even more collaboration utilities within Office at your disposal. Skype also has an app available in the Windows Store and Microsoft has announced that Skype will replace Windows Messenger altogether soon.

- **Sharing**   All Office 2013 apps have a Share item on their File tab through which you can invite people to view and edit documents on your SkyDrive—whether they have Office 2013 or not.

- **SkyDrive saving by default**   After you set up a SkyDrive account with Office 2013, Office apps will by default save to the cloud instead of on your computer. Naturally, you can choose to save to your computer instead, but saving to SkyDrive does enable easier sharing of documents via the Share option on the File tab in any given Office 2013 app.

- **OneNote**   OneNote is the single application in Office that has a version in the Windows Store that uses the Windows 8–style interface—all other Office 2013 apps are desktop-only apps.

As shown in Figure 14-3, the OneNote Windows Store app uses what's called a radial menu, which is a circular version of a context menu that combines commands in a circular fashion, with outward pointing arrows that contain more options. Further, OneNote has versions available on Android and iOS devices. Microsoft, by doing this, seems to believe so much in OneNote that it would rather support competitor devices than squander OneNote's potential. You can find OneNote's Windows 8–style version after installing Office 2013 in the Windows Store under Productivity apps.

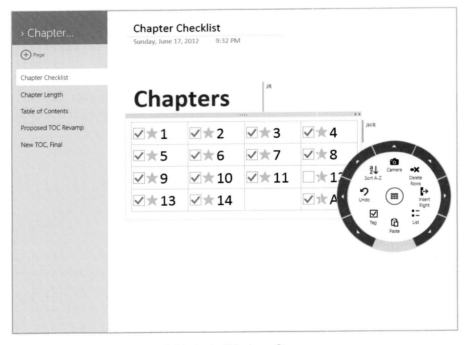

Figure 14-3   *OneNote is available in the Windows Store.*

Extend Office 2013 with Office 365

Office 365 is Microsoft's cloud-based complement to the Office 2013 suite. Office 365 is a subscription model that extends the Office 2013 apps to other computers. If you have an Office 365 subscription, for example, and are on a computer that doesn't have Office installed on it, you can log in to your Office 365 account and stream a version of the Office app you need over the Internet to do your editing.

Index